Eat the Bankers

The Case Against Usury:

The Root Cause of the Economic Crisis and the Fix

By Sinclair Noe

I0475500

NSA Educational Publishing

Los Angeles, CA

ISBN 1452823731

Library of Congress Cataloging-in-Publication Data applied for

Noe, Sinclair

    Eat the bankers: the case against usury: the root cause of the economic crisis and the fix/ Sinclair Noe
Finance. 2. Usury 3. Banking

Printed in the United States of America

To Teca, with love

and

Thanks to Paul

Contents

The Case Against Usury

Introduction

What if there was an economic system that did not experience booms and busts, inflation and deflation, recessions and depressions? What if there was an economic system that promised universal prosperity? There is. The laws of this marvelous economic system have been laid out by virtually every society. The guidelines for this beneficent and harmonious economic system were given to us more than 4,000 years ago; the rules are more relevant and necessary than ever. What is this miraculous economic system? It is simply to eliminate usury. When we see the violent results of modern economic experiments wouldn't it make sense to consider the ancient God given wisdom which promises social and economic justice and abundance?

Bankers are evil. They are unrepentant. The bankers have pulled off the biggest theft in history and they continue to steal: jobs, value, sweat, blood, dignity, hard earned dollars, democracy, and freedom. Their assault weapon is usury, and it is a sin.

We are not alone. Our bravest heroes were also robbed. Sometimes it's hard to make ends meet. This is especially true for the brave men and women who rely on a military paycheck; sometimes they fall into the debt trap. The Pentagon says excessive debt hurts troop morale and poses a potential security risk. Congress recognized the problem and rode to the rescue, enacting the 2007 National Defense Authorization Act. Among other things, the Act protected US troops from becoming the targets of predatory lenders. The Act made it illegal for lenders to accept military paychecks or car titles to secure high interest loans, sometimes at annual interest rates that topped 400%. Many of the lenders get loans from the Federal Reserve for less than 0.5%; they then jack up the rates for consumers. The Act made it illegal, with certain exemptions, to charge active military personnel more than 36% annual interest rates on consumer loans. Mission accomplished.

One year later, Bear Sterns and Merrill Lynch were taken under by competitors. Lehman Brothers was allowed to collapse. The largest savings and loan, Washington Mutual was gobbled up by JPMorgan Chase. The fourth largest bank, Wachovia was scooped up by Citigroup and then eventually taken over by Wells Fargo. The largest mortgage originator, Countrywide, was taken under by Bank of America. IndyMac and other smaller banks were taken over by the FDIC. Congress approved legislation based upon a three-page ransom note scribbled by Treasury Secretary Henry Paulson, which opened the vaults of the US Treasury and handed over more than $700 billion to treasonous, larcenous bankers.

In October 2008, a poll showed 90% of Americans thought the country was headed in the wrong direction. They were right. Money was printed and spent at a furious pace but it didn't filter down to average families. Jobs are still hard to find and easy to lose; and once a job is lost it might never return. The cost of living keeps going up while the standard of living goes down. Around the world, poverty plagues more than 3 billion people worldwide, half the planet. America is now the largest debtor nation in history, the kind of distinction once reserved for banana republics. We are now stuck in a not so great depression. The middle class in America is less concerned with climbing the ladder of success than falling off the ladder and dropping into the pit of poverty.

By mid-2009, the price of the bailout grew to $2.5 trillion spent, with another $12 trillion to $24 trillion committed. All that money helped prop up Wall Street and the global financial system still teetered on the verge of meltdown; despite the greatest redistribution of wealth in history.

What went wrong? How did we get so far off track?

It is both easy and accurate to say that greed is the cause of the failure. We know that the love of money is the root of all evil, but that doesn't provide answers to why we have seen such a massive collapse and how we can pull ourselves out of the hole.

The problems can be traced back to a single root cause, a blunt axe that chops away at our incomes, our savings, the economy, and our freedom – usury.

Most people do not even know the meaning of the word "usury". The definition is: interest or gain paid on a loan.

That means any increase, any premium, any gain, or any interest on any loan. Over time that definition seemed too strict. The law recognized that interest is commonly collected on a loan. Countries and states set limits on usury. The legal definition for usury came to be known as the interest rate above the legal limit.

We have gutted the usury laws in the past 30 years. We have had our collective intelligence purged of the concept of usury. Most people who know what usury means associate it with a loan shark, a sleazy caricature willing to bash kneecaps to collect on a loan. Today the usurer/loan sharks wear suits, work in office buildings, and have national bank charters. The bankers are doing things that would make Tony Soprano blush. Usury infects our entire economy in ways no street criminal could imagine. For the past 30 years, the country has tried a radical experiment that embraced usury and the results are catastrophic. Usury has created volatile markets, increased inflation, allowed the usurers (people who collect the gains on a loan) to buy influence in government, subverted democracy, centralized wealth, created economic disparity, decimated the middle class, discouraged productivity, sent jobs off-shore, and pushed the country into a new depression. Now, we think of usury as excessive or outrageous interest on a loan. The problem is that bankers don't know the meaning of the word "excessive".

How's this for excessive? More people have lost their homes to foreclosure than at any time since the Great Depression. Many of the same troops that risked their lives in Iraq and Afghanistan came back from war to find their homes were being lost to foreclosure. The sharp axe that chops the feet out from under our bravest heroes is usury; swinging that axe – bankers. It's really not new. In the days of the Civil War, Abraham Lincoln gave this honest assessment of the real enemies of the Union: "The money powers prey on the nation in times of peace and conspire against it in times of adversity. The banking powers are more despotic than monarchy, more insolent than autocracy, more selfish than bureaucracy. They denounce as public enemies all who question their methods or throw light upon their crimes. I have two great enemies, the Southern Army in front of me, and the bankers in the rear. Of the two, the one at my rear is my greatest foe. As a most undesirable consequence of the war, corporations have been enthroned, and an era of corruption in high places will follow. The money power will endeavor to prolong its reign by working upon the prejudices of the people until the wealth is aggregated in the hands of a few, and the Republic is destroyed."

Today America is fighting two wars but the greatest danger still comes from the enemies to the rear – the bankers, because we've turned our backs on the collective wisdom of 4,000 years. Usury has been around ever since people have been borrowing property or money; and for most of history usury has been considered a big problem, a mortal sin comparable to murder, and so evil that there is a special place in hell for usurers.

Only in the last 30 years have we abandoned prohibitions and limits on usury. We have, for all practical purposes, legalized usury and excessive interest. We haven't even stopped to consider whether there might be problems that arise from this radical acceptance of usury. This brief experiment has proven catastrophic. The bankers sold us a story that material wealth can grow exponentially and infinitely. The truth is that only debt can grow exponentially and infinitely, but nothing else in the natural world grows like debt, with the possible exception of cancer, but even there the host is put out of his misery.

Usury is condemned on moral, religious, and ethical grounds. All major religions condemn usury, yet today most people, even those that consider themselves devoutly religious, practice usury. Great civilizations have thrived while prohibiting or limiting usury. Throughout history, usury has been considered a root cause of social injustice, economic instability, inflation, disparity, inequality, violence, war, and poverty.

There is a direct relationship between usury and the current economic problems. Trade-offs were made, legislation was rewritten, rules were deregulated, laws ignored, and our democracy has been undermined; it did not happen in one dramatic act, but slowly and insidiously. The rise in usury led directly to predatory loans, foreclosures, personal and business bankruptcy, debts that spiral out of control and never seem to get paid despite good intentions. Many families have suffered quietly, blaming themselves for what was happening. Bankers have no moral compass. They reject compassion and try to shift culpability. Shame turns to anger as people realize that bankers were handing out predatory, misleading, false, and usurious debt like a pedophile offering candy to a child. We don't blame the child for taking the candy.

Usury traps the most desperate; it is a form of regressive taxation that chops away at the middle class and working poor. Usury enslaves the borrower and oppresses the poor. Peasant farmers in ancient Greece were forced into slavery when they could not pay their debts. Monarchies have a long history of economic enslavement of their subjects. America was a radical concept in 1776, because We the People were more important than the nobility and the elite few. Today's corporate nobility is no different than the monarchs, oligarchs, and tyrants of old. Leopards don't change their spots.

Usury wasted a great economy by shifting investment capital away from productive purposes. Money seeks the greatest return, and manufacturing and entrepreneurial enterprise can't compete with the hefty returns of usury. Money has been sucked out of the middle class and centralized in the hands of an elite few, redistributed from willing hands of practical purpose to add to the abundance of those who already have more than enough. Without restrictions, the economy has gone through one crash after another, and incalculable damage has been done to individuals and our country.

Usury stunts economic development and perpetuates poverty. Bailing out the financial system has come with an astronomical price tag. This is money that could have been used for productive purposes; this is money that could have created jobs; this is money that could have eliminated worldwide poverty in our lifetime. Instead, this is money that has been sucked into the dark, bottomless hole that is the bankers' pockets. We had a chance to try to achieve worldwide prosperity versus extravagant lifestyles for an elite few. A choice was made and it will be the lasting legacy of this generation, but it is not too late to change that legacy.

It may be too much to imagine that we can eliminate all interest, but it is pure insanity to accept excessive usury. The fundamental right of people to be protected from exploitation if they seek credit must be reasserted. Equity, financial fairness, and caps on excessive interest rates are not new concepts. Until laws against usury were repealed in 1980, in most situations and in most states, it was illegal to charge more than about 10%. Somehow banks survived before 1980; somehow bankers made a good living without multi-million dollar bonuses; somehow the US was the most productive economy in the history of the world before we abandoned restrictions on usury; somehow we have fallen.

The root cause of our problems can be traced to usury. The solution to our problems will come from putting an end to usury.

How to Read this Book

This book is divided into five sections.

The first section covers the history of usury and explains how all major religions and great philosophers denounce usury. I do not claim to be a theologian but it would be ridiculous to ignore the religious teachings on this subject. I have included a few brief citations of scripture in this section. The Appendix includes further scriptural citations for those who want to pursue this line further. It would be impossible to cite all the religious, philosophic, and economic arguments against usury stretching back more than 4,000 years. The greatest minds in history had clear moral, ethical, and economic objections to usury.

The second section covers more recent history, from the Great Depression to our current depression, and explains how interest rate controls began disappearing in this country beginning in 1978. The media has not had much coverage of this fundamental shift in the economy, the politicians were willing accomplices, and the banks got away with murder – taking the global economy to the edge of collapse.

The third section explores the usury-caused damage to families, individuals, businesses and communities. This section covers the growth of consumer debt through credit cards, payday loans, and predatory mortgages.

The fourth section deals with the economic ramifications of usury; how usury has caused inflation and shifted capital from productive purpose, pushed jobs offshore; centralized wealth and created ever increasing disparity; how usury has lead to boom-bust cycles; how usury places an unfair burden on the middle class; how usury has created a regressive tax policy; how the largest tax on most Americans is the cost of usury; and how usury has become the fuel of war and violence.

The final section presents a 12 step solution to the unsustainable usury model and many of the myths surrounding our current usurious system are debunked. It is unrealistic to expect that all interest can be eliminated. The exact line between excessive and reasonable interest rates can be debated. The path to acceptable interest rates can be debated. The political and social changes required to achieve fair interest rates can be debated. What is not debatable is that today's excessive interest rates are dangerous and indefensible.

Section One

How Ignoring 4,000 Years of Economic Wisdom Has Led Us to the Brink

Chapter 1

Usury – Does Anybody Remember the Primary Economic Principle?

Usury comes from the Latin word usuria, meaning interest. The definition is interest, premium, gain, or charge for the use of money in any circumstance; or interest charged above legal limits; or interest charged at excessive rates.

The distinction between usury and interest is wholly civic and legal. What is usury in one country or state is merely interest in another. If the laws forbid the taking of any increase on loans, then all interest would be usury. Perhaps the best definition came from Blackstone's Commentaries on English Law: "When money is lent on a contract to receive not only the principal sum again, but also an increase by way of compensation for the use, the increase is called interest by those who think it lawful, and usury by those who do not."

It's important to start with the basic definition of usury because the majority of Americans do not know the word; in the past thirty years it has been nearly erased from our collective knowledge and conscience. The first economic principle is "thou shall not steal"; the corollary is that usury is theft. John M. Keynes, perhaps the most influential economist of the last century, said, "Provisions against usury are amongst the most ancient economic practices of which we have record." Remarkably, we fail to see this ancient wisdom can guide us to economic recovery.

Anyone who has ever read the fine print of a loan contract knows gains are frequently disguised. Gains can include fees, leverage, fractional reserves, and insurance; the more gains are tacked on, the riskier the loan. The higher the hurdle is set, the more difficult it is to jump over. Every loan shark knows excessive gains for the lender increase the risk of default.

For most of history the taking of any charge on the use of money was considered usury, and usury was a grave sin, comparable to theft or even worse. The philosopher Cato, in *De Re Rustica*, was asked, "And what do you think of usury?" and his reply was, "What do you think of murder?"

Usury was condemned and reviled by all major religions: Christianity, Islam, Hinduism, Buddhism, and Judaism. Usury was further condemned by the greatest philosophers, politicians, and leaders in history including: Aristotle, Plato, Cato, Cicero, Seneca, Aquinas, Solomon, Charlemagne, Milton, Dante, Shakespeare, Bacon, Benjamin Franklin, Thomas Jefferson, and Andrew Jackson. In fourteenth century England, the taking of any interest was a capital crime. At various times in history usurers have faced penalties ranging from the confiscation of their wealth, exile, excommunication, prison, mob violence, or even death.

It was a very serious offense to collect *any* interest on a loan. Over time the definition was diluted to the more modern concept of charging excessive interest. One of the main justifications for allowing *some* interest was the need to finance wars and empire building.

Despite near universal condemnation, usury slowly and surely crept into common acceptance. Today, it is rare to hear criticism of usury in a church, synagogue, mosque or temple. This is sad because the family and finance are interconnected. Man as an economic being cannot be abstracted from other aspects of life. Every house of worship includes the faithful whose faith is tested by economic stress. The Golden Rule applies to all religions and it is not just an educational tool for children, it is a core principle for commerce and life. To ignore usury is to become the people Jesus warned us about.

Philosophers can't begin to address social injustice without recognizing that "poverty is the worst form of violence" (-Gandhi) and "debt is the worst form of poverty" (-Lichtwer). Economists seem to enjoy making simple things sound complex. The most powerful economic formula is compound interest, yet economists seem to flit around the edges of this concept. They tend to look past the 8-ton elephant in the room, distracted by the peanuts. Political leaders avoid usury like the plague. They think their job security depends on campaign contributions. They delude themselves that they can accept bribes and still represent the People. They lie when they say they are serving one master while collecting money from another. When politicians serve the bankers and not the people, we face the destruction of democracy.

Chapter 2

Religious Criticism of Usury – What Would Buddha, Krishna, Moses, Mohammed, and Jesus Do?

The earliest religious criticism of usury dates back 4,000 years. The Hindu Vedic texts from ancient India describe *kusidin*, or usurers, as lenders who charge any interest. Vashishtha prohibited priests and warriors from lending for interest. The Sutra describes several references to payment of interest. By the second century AD the definition of usury was softened to imply any interest beyond the legal rate.

The Holy Quran strictly prohibits usury, or *riba*. It is written in the Holy Quran: "Those who devour usury will not stand except as stand one whom the Satan by his touch hath driven to madness." (2.275), "Allah will deprive usury of all blessing." (2.276), and "As for those who persist in usury, they incur Hell, wherein they abide forever." (2.275)

It is widely believed that Islam prohibits all interest, but there is a segment of Islamic thought that argues that usury only applies to loans made for consumptive purposes, while interest may be applied to loans for commercial investment. There is no debate that the Prophet Mohammed denounced usury in his teachings.

Of course, there were always loopholes. Delayment fees, mohatra contracts (or repurchase agreements), and the contractum trinius (a three-part contract where the lender would make an investment, insure the amount of the investment, and then sell any profits to the would-be borrower) were widely used throughout both the Christian and Muslim worlds, and effectively replicated interest-bearing contracts. The banning of usury complicated, but did not end, debt finance. The ban was eventually repealed, after the revision of the doctrine by the School of Salamanca and the gradual lifting of laws in Protestant countries in the mid-1600s.

An entire system of interest-free financial institutions now serves much of the Muslim world. Islamic banking is based upon usury-free financing principles including joint ventures and profit sharing plans. Mortgages can be handled by the bank buying a property and allowing installment payments by the people living in and purchasing the property.

The advantages of Islamic banking include a closer relationship between the bank and the client which results in less risk to the lender and more responsible and ultimately more profitable loans. With increased due diligence there is less volatility, more stability for the banks, and more equitable distribution of resources. Islamic banking is not without problems; the due diligence is sometimes considered excessive and requires endorsements from different boards that interpret Sharia law as it applies to the project and transaction. Systems and products lack uniformity from institution to institution and from country to country. Some argue that bank participation in profit or loss is just a roundabout way of collecting interest. The counter argument is that the lender has "skin in the game", as opposed to the Western view that the lender gets paid even when the enterprise loses. Islam permits trade but forbids usury, in part because trade is the result of initiative, enterprise, and efficiency. *Riba*, or interest, is considered surplus gain without counterpart value.

Judaism has forbidden and discouraged usury. The Hebrew word for interest is *neshek*, which translates to bite, like the bite of a serpent. It is a fitting word because the venom from a snake bite spreads out and diffuses until it reaches the nervous system and vital organs, likewise the increase in usury starts out small and grows to devour a person's substance.

There are numerous Biblical passages that clearly prohibit usury. Ex. 22:25: "If thou lend money to any of my people that is poor by thee, thou shalt not be to him as a usurer, neither shalt thou lay upon him usury."

There are many other prohibitions against usury, however for Jewish and Christian apologists for usury there appears to be a loophole: Deut. 23:19,20: "Thou shalt not lend upon usury to thy brother; usury of money, usury of victuals, usury of anything that is lent upon usury. Unto a stranger thou mayest lend upon usury; but unto they brother thou shalt not lend upon usury; that the Lord thy God may bless thee in all that thou settest thine hand to in the land whither thou goest to possess it." The broadest interpretation here is that usury was allowed by Jews dealing with non-Jews (strangers) but was not allowed when dealing with fellow Jews (brothers).

This loophole is closed shut in other scripture: Lev. 25:35,36: "And if a brother be waxen poor, and fallen in decay with thee, then thou shalt relieve him: yea, though he be a stranger, or a sojourner; that he may live with thee. Take thou no usury of him, or increase: but fear thy God; that thy brother may live with thee." Also, Ex. 23:9: "Also thou shalt not oppress a stranger: for ye know the heart of a stranger, seeing ye were strangers in the land of Egypt."

The prophet Ezekiel considered "usury or increase" an abomination and comparable to fraud, violence, impurity, and idolatry. When there is fraud without dishonesty, and violence without injury, and adultery without impurity, and idolatry without false worship, then may there be "usury and increase" without injustice and oppression.

Despite the prohibition of usury there is considerable evidence to suggest that this rule was not always observed. Nothing more clearly marked the line between Jews and Christians during fifteen centuries than this one thing, that Jews exacted usury or interest from Gentiles, while Christianity forbade the practice.

The prohibition of usury was binding during the reigns of David and Solomon. The ships of King Solomon entered every port in the known world, but usury was never a part of the commerce in that prosperous time.

Christianity built upon the Old Testament prohibitions of usury with New Testament fervor. It is out of harmony with the life and teachings of Jesus that he should encourage or permit a means of increasing wealth forbidden by the laws given by Moses and classified as abominations and sins by the prophets.

The first disciples did not loan but gave to those in need: Rom. 13:8: "Owe no man anything, but to love one another:"

There was no question about the disciples' dedication: Matt. 6:24: "No one can serve two masters. He will either hate one and love the other, or be devoted to one and despise the other. You cannot serve God and mammon." Some versions reference: "You cannot serve God and money." Christ counsels to make our best things the joys and glories of the other world, those things not seen which are eternal, and to place our happiness in them. The worldly man is wrong in his first principle; therefore all his justifications and resultant actions must be wrong.

The strongest rejection of loans at interest came from Christ in Luke 6:35: "Lend, hoping for nothing in return."

The teachings of Jesus were, in large part, about love, peace, forgiveness, compassion, and service to others, especially those less fortunate. He was known to lend his hand to the poor, the sick, foreigners, prostitutes, and sinners – yet there is one instance where the Prince of Peace turned to violence; one instance where he destroyed property; one instance where he took a whip to another man – when he chased the money changers from the Temple. Matt 21:12: "And Jesus entered the temple of God and drove out all who sold and bought in the temple and turned the tables of the money changers and the seats of those who sold pigeons. He said to them, It is written, My house show be called a house of prayer; but you make it a den of robbers."

Also, John 2:15 – "and he made a scourge of cords, and cast all out of the temple, both the sheep and the oxen; and he poured out the changers' money, and overthrew their tables…"

This example of civil disobedience goes beyond the non-violent code. Jesus forgave the soldiers that crucified him on the cross, but He did not forgive the usurers in the Temple. Many people use a simple question as a moral compass: what would Jesus do? We know what He did with the bankers of His time. He turned to violence.

The Roman Catholic Church was emphatic in its condemnation of usury. Clergy was prohibited from taking usury by the fourth century; the prohibition was also extended to the laity. The Encyclopedia of Religious Knowledge says: "All the apostolic fathers condemned the taking of usury." St. John Chrysostom said: "Nothing is baser in this world than usury, nothing more cruel."

Saints Tertullian, Cyprian, Ambrose, Augustine, and Jerome can be quoted in their condemnation against usury. The popes followed the teachings of the fathers and imposed severe penalties. Priests guilty of this sin were degraded from their orders; laymen found guilty were excommunicated. Interest paid could be reclaimed, not only from the usurer but from his heirs. In the eighth century, Charlemagne, in France, made usury a general criminal offence.

A council at Westminster, in 1126, decided that all clergy who were guilty of practicing usury should be degraded. Archbishop Sands said: "This canker, usury, hath corrupted all of England."

In 1311, Pope Clement V made the prohibition of usury absolute and wiped out all secular legislation in its favor, and a council in Vienna reaffirmed the denunciations: "If any shall obstinately persist in the error of presuming to affirm that the taking of usury is not a sin, we decree that he shall be punished as a heretic." There is no record of the repeal of any of these edicts.

Usury proved a difficult temptation to deny. By 1465, Pope Paul II approved *mons pietatis*, "poor men's banks", the early version of pawn shops. These nonprofit banks lent to the deserving poor at very low rates of interest, and by the late fifteenth century, they began to accept deposits. By the sixteenth century these banks were spread by the Franciscans all over Europe, though not in England, where Parliament refused to legalize them.

As commerce spread, the debate grew. The early 1500's saw challenges to the authority of the Church. Both Luther and Calvin opposed usury. Luther was vehement in his opposition. Calvin expressed some reservations. Luther said: "Whoever eats up, robs and steals the nourishment of another, commits as great a murder, as he who carves a man or utterly undoes him. Such does a usurer, and he sits the while on his stool, when he ought rather to be hanging from the gallows."

John Calvin's letter on usury of 1545 made it clear that when Christ said "lend hoping for nothing in return," He meant that we should help the poor freely. Calvin acknowledged that "it is very rare for a man to be honest and yet a usurer." Calvin expressed his opposition to usury and then relented: "It could be wished that all usury and the name itself were first banished from the earth. But as this cannot be accomplished it should be seen what can be done for the public good." And he decided: "usury is not wholly forbidden among us unless it be repugnant both to Charity and Justice." Even though Calvin enumerated seven examples where usury remained sinful, his position was considered as encouragement for taking interest.

By 1745, the rhetoric softened substantially. Pope Benedict XIV wrote an encyclical saying: "One cannot condone the sin of usury by arguing that the gain is not great or excessive, but rather moderate or small;" but then he added a loophole: "We do not deny that at times together with the loan contract certain other titles - which are not at all intrinsic to the contract - may run parallel with it. From these other titles, entirely just and legitimate reasons arise to demand something over and above the amount due on the contract. Nor is it denied that it is very often possible for someone, by means of contracts differing entirely from loans, to spend and invest money legitimately either to provide oneself with an annual income or to engage in legitimate trade and business. From these types of contracts honest gain may be made."

In 1891, Pope Leo XIII spoke of "voracious usury" which he described as: "an evil condemned frequently by the Church but nevertheless still practiced in deceptive ways by avaricious men."

In 2005, Pope Benedict XVI condemned the "deplorable social plague of usury". There was no question that the current definition of usury referred to "excessive interest". In the 2009 encyclical, *Truth in Charity*, Benedict wrote, "The weakest members of society should be helped to defend themselves against usury".

Usury has always been and will always be a sin.

Chapter 3

Philosophers and Leaders – What is Money? Why is Usury Wrong?

Usury became a problem in ancient Greece shortly after the introduction of coins. Before the widespread use of coins a farmer would borrow various commodities to plant his crops and he would repay the loan with the harvest. When coins were introduced the farmer had to borrow money to buy supplies; the commodities were in high demand and priced high at planting season; at harvest time the commodities were plentiful and priced low. The farmers could not pay back the loans; they lost their farms and land ownership became concentrated in the hands of the elite, or oligarchs. The farmers were subjected to slavery.

Around 600 BC, Solon introduced the idea of *Seisachtheia*, which means shaking off burdens or debts. Solon canceled debt contracts, returned farm land to peasant farmers, ruled that slavery could no longer be used to enforce debt contracts, and set minimum prices for agricultural products. Solon did not set a limit on interest rates, but his reforms seemed to keep usury under check.

Meanwhile, in Rome there was a similar situation; the peasant farmers were falling into debt. Rome set limits on interest rates without changing the laws on debt. Outlying provinces still faced ridiculous usury, and bad debt often resulted in slavery, more or less, for the borrower. Julius Caesar eventually adopted the legislation of Solon, and in 88 BC, interest rates were set at a maximum of 12%, but by then the Roman middle class had been effectively destroyed. Eventually, Justinian set rates at 6% and 8% for mercantile loans.

Aristotle formulated what is considered a classic case against usury. Religious leaders had already denounced usury as a *malum in se*, a sin in and of itself. Aristotle understood usury to be a sin because it was a type of theft. Aristotle explained why it was also a sin against nature. Money is sterile and according to Aristotle it exists not by nature but by law. Because usury forces money to breed more money it was a perversion of the natural process of procreation because only natural organisms can procreate. Aristotle used the word *tokos* to define usury, but the word also meant offspring, or birth. Usury became associated with sexual perversion. The poet Dante would later take that association a step further, placing those who have committed sins against nature, sodomites, blasphemers, and usurers, on the same metaphysical plane – the seventh circle of Hell.

Aristotle argued that money is a store of value. It represents a good or service produced. Money, in and of itself, does not produce anything of value. Usury allows someone to gain wealth without working for it. According to Aristotle: "The trade of the petty usurer is hated with most reason: it makes a profit from currency itself, instead of making it from the process which currency was meant to serve. Their common characteristic is obviously their sordid avarice."

Taking the idea a step further, the usurer can have no rightful claim to any portion of the labor of the borrower, without surrendering some portion of his property back to the borrower as compensation for services received. This was the problem faced by the peasant farmers in ancient Athens; the farmers provided all the labor to work the fields but kept none of the fruits of their labor. The conditions found in ancient Athens are not so different from today. Entrepreneurs struggle under the burden of debt, sacrificing profits to pay the bankers, impoverishing their own families to enrich the bankers. If the businessperson fails, he fails; if the banker fails, the businessperson must bail him out.

It is legitimate to think of interest as profit only when it is participation in profits, but when there is no participation in production, when it merely finances current consumption, it is wealth without work, growing rich without adding anything useful to society; indeed, it is growing rich by sucking value out of society; no better than a parasite or a cancer.

St. Thomas Aquinas was one of the Church scholars known as Scholastics (1100 -1500 AD) who created the study of economics, and their main concern was usury. St. Thomas quotes Aristotle as saying that "to live by usury is exceedingly unnatural". Aquinas argued money's function is to measure the fruits of economic activity – it is a medium of exchange. Money is a measure of things that are sold – it is a store of value. But money, in and of itself, does not create the fruits of economic activity. Money is not itself a commodity that can be sold. Aquinas essentially said that your money, once spent is used up. Aquinas argued that it was morally wrong for someone to sell a cake, charge for the cake, and then charge again for the person to actually eat the cake. This was double billing or theft.

Aquinas further argued that usury was a method of selling time – the repayment of usury must be paid with the energy and time of the borrower. But time only belonged to God, so not only was usury a type of theft; it was stealing from God himself.

Lending at interest for guaranteed returns, with no risk and no work, was a sin, but it was also agreed that if the lender shared in the profit and the risk, the loan was legal; this was the idea of a joint venture, which is still acceptable today in Islamic banking. Commerce, with attendant risks and rewards, was not a sin. Over time it became acceptable to charge for losses because the borrower was using money. The difference between the amount loaned and the profit the lender might have made, was charged as interest - if it could be proved that there was a lost opportunity to make money. Contracts also included penalties for late payment.

In Italy, the Medici family built large and powerful banks; they did not charge interest on loans but they did accept gifts from their clients. Change the metaphor and you change the opinion. It was no longer usury, it was interest. Usury was sinful, interest was a benign gift.

The basic question of the philosophers and early economists really boiled down to, "What is money?" Money has assumed different forms and shapes: coins, salt, tally sticks, seashells, furs, feathers, wheels, coconuts, paper, beads, plastic, and digital entries – all have been used as money. Money is anything that people will accept in exchange for goods or services, in the belief that they may in turn exchange it, now or later, for other goods or services.

Money is a medium of exchange. Money is a measure of value. Goods and services are produced by people. Money does not produce goods and services. Usury is a scheme to use money to create more money, but it does not create goods, services, or anything of value; therefore, usury steals part of the value from the people that did produce goods and services. Usury steals from the future to pay for the present.

The first bank of deposit and discount was the Bank of Venice. The bank began its association with the Republic of Venetia in 1171; both the bank and the republic collapsed in 1797. The republic was impoverished following war with the Emperor of Greece. The republic forced the citizens to make a loan to the state. In return, the citizens were given stock in the bank. Stock in the bank was a loan to the state at four percent annually. Eventually all payments for everything was handled by the bank, entered as credits by the Chamber of Commissions. The bank issued credits backed by pure gold ducats, which replaced other gold and silver coins. The bank credits were convenient and easy to use. The bank demanded and received a premium for credits; credits weren't worth more than gold; the premium collected did not add productive value to the Venetian economy, it just made the rich richer and the poor poorer. Venetia started as a pure republican democracy, electing a ruling leader, or Doge, and council to represent the citizens; but as the bank grew, so did the bank's involvement in government; democracy gave way to councils which represented the bank. Representative government became less so, shrinking to a Council of Ten, then a Tribunal of Three. Over a period of 600 years, the wealth of Venice was centralized and democracy faded.

By the late sixteenth century, usury was increasingly tolerated despite pragmatic opposition. In 1569, Thomas Wilson wrote *A Discourse Upon Usurye*: "Usury overthrows trade, decays merchandise, undoes tillage, destroys craftsmen, defaces chivalries, beats down nobility, brings dearth and famine, and causes destruction and confusion."

Theologians remained opposed to usury, but commerce and law ruled; usury was allowed if the loan was made with good intentions. Who determined good intentions? It was generally left to individuals to decide if their intentions and actions were sinful. Still there were limits. In 1571, England set a maximum interest rate of 10%, labeled *An Act Against Usury*, the aim was to lessen the exploitative part of usury by making it legal. England had already established certain limits on usury in the Magna Carta. In 1624, the Parliament passed the *Act Against Usury* and lowered the maximum rate to 8% per annum, but the loans still could only be made in good conscience. This of course led to secular debate about state control on matters of conscience, but with interest rates falling, the debate lost steam.

In 1689, William and Mary began their reign over the Kingdom of England, but only by taking out a loan of 1,200,000 pounds sterling. The loan was never meant to be repaid, but interest at the rate of eight percent per year was to be paid forever. The loan created the Bank of England and the Bank has held the purse strings to the kingdom since that time, privately run and generally impervious to direction; the monarchs became the servants of the Bank. The Bank in turn financed the empire, but always at a cost. At the beginning of the 21st century, Britons were still paying off debts from the Napoleonic Wars. The creation of the Bank of England provided state sanctioned legitimacy to usury. "The bank hath benefit of interest on all moneys which it creates out of nothing." - William Paterson, founder of the Bank of England in 1694.

Even though usury grew to be accepted, it was still denounced. Shakespeare mocked the usurer Shylock in the Merchant of Venice. In Hamlet, Polonius advised: "Neither a borrower nor a lender be."

The Dutch determined that bankers were a seedy lot: "Bankers were excluded from communion by an ordinance of 1581, joining a list of other shady occupations---pawnbrokers, actors, jugglers, acrobats, quacks, and brothel keepers---that were disqualified from receiving God's grace. Their wives were permitted to join the Lord's Supper, but only on condition that they publicly declared their repugnance for their husband's profession! Their families shared the taint and were only permitted to join communion after a public profession of distaste for dealing in money. It was not until 1658 that the States of Holland (the representatives of the estates of nobles and commoners to the court of Holland) persuaded the church to withdraw this humiliating prohibition on Lombards."

Francis Bacon acknowledged the sin of usury: "They say that it is a pity the devil should have God's part, which is the tithe. That the usurer is the greatest Sabbath-breaker, because his plough goeth every Sunday." Bacon then looked at arguments for and against usury. The argument against usury was that it made fewer merchants, and wealth was idled and not used for productive purposes, also it centralized wealth, and stifled innovation. The argument for usury was that the practice provided capital for enterprises, it was good to have the ability to borrow in times of catastrophe or emergency, and finally nobody will lend unless they can take a profit. This final argument for usury was pragmatic; usury is permitted because the usurers can get away with it. Under this logic, murder would be acceptable when the murderer is not caught and tried. Bacon concludes that usury must be allowed, but at a low rate, maximum 5%, which would force capital to look for higher returns from agriculture or manufacturing.

Adam Smith was a Scottish philosopher and is widely considered the father of modern economics. In 1776, in the *Wealth of Nations* Smith advocated limits on usury:

"The legal rate...ought not be much above the lowest market rate. If the legal rate of interest in Great Britain, for example, was fixed so high as eight or ten per cent, the greater part of the money which was to be lent would be lent to prodigals and projectors (promoters of fraudulent schemes), who alone would be willing to give this high interest....A great part of the capital of the country would thus be kept out of the hands which were most likely to make a profitable and advantageous use of it, and thrown into those which were most likely to waste and destroy it. When the legal rate of interest, on the contrary is fixed but a very little above the lowest market rate, sober people are universally preferred, as borrowers, to prodigals and projectors. The person who lends money gets nearly as much interest from the former as he dares to take from the latter, and his money is much safer in the hands of the one set of people than in those of the other. A great part of the capital of the country is thus thrown in the hands in which it is most likely to be employed with advantage."

It almost seems that Adam Smith was foretelling the breakdown of the derivatives and credit markets, as well as the subprime crisis that would hit 230 years after he wrote these words.

Public, artistic, philosophical, political, and economic opposition to usury could not stand up to the new, more powerful form of usury that was created out of the central banking scheme. Central banking worked on the principle of fractional reserves, an old trick learned by goldsmiths and money changers. The money changers would often hold gold or other metals as deposits, for a fee, and issue receipts or paper notes. The notes were accepted for many commercial transactions. The money changers and goldsmiths quickly discovered they could make loans based upon deposits held, and the loans were made in the form of paper notes. They figured they could issue more paper notes than the actual gold deposits held in reserve, because it was unlikely that all depositors would demand their gold at the same time. They issued notes based upon gold reserves even though there wasn't enough gold to fully back the notes; they were creating money out of thin air.

This was another form of usury, souped up, faster, and more powerful. The usurer/central bank could take in $10 dollars in gold deposits and issue $100 dollars in loans in the form of paper notes. Note that the usurer/central bank used other people's deposited money to create loans. Assuming a 10% interest rate, the interest charged on $100 would be $10 dollars. The usurer/central bank started with $10 and collected $10 in interest; the real interest rate was 100%.

Now there was $100 dollars in paper notes circulating through the economy, not just $10 in gold – more dollars but the same amount of products that could be bought - the result was inevitable: inflation, booms, and busts. Even the prudent citizen, who avoided borrowing or lending, now paid a higher price because of fractional reserve lending. The borrower had to repay $110 dollars, which means he had to increase his output by 10% just to repay the principle and interest; even then, any profit above the principle and interest was worth less because each dollar had been devalued by inflation. The businessperson had to increase his output even more if he hoped to increase his standard of living.

This is the basic blueprint for central banking. The plan is essentially unchanged over the past nine centuries. All governments have the inherent power to create their own currency. One of the great unanswered questions of the past thousand years is: why the hell do we need central banks acting as middlemen to create currency?

Chapter 4

Early America – The Little Tax on Tea; The Enemies to the Rear

The pre-Revolutionary United States enjoyed a prosperous and growing economy. Benjamin Franklin captured the economic essence of his time with succinct and memorable lines: "a penny saved is a penny earned," and "he who goes a-borrowing goes a-sorrowing." Franklin provided more in-depth analysis in his autobiography: "In the Colonies we issue our own money. It is called Colonial Script. We issue it in proper proportion to the demands of trade and industry to make the products pass easily from the producers to the consumers. In this manner, creating for ourselves our own paper money, we control its purchasing power, and we have no interest to pay to no one." – Benjamin Franklin.

Colonial Script was made illegal by the Currency Act of 1764. The Bank of England assumed control of currency for the colonies, and the Bank of England imposed usury, and the crown imposed taxes. Economic depression resulted. Franklin explained what happened next: "In one year, the conditions were so reversed that the era of prosperity ended, and a depression set in, to such an extent that the streets of the Colonies were filled with unemployed. The colonies would gladly have borne the little tax on tea and other matters had it not been that England took away from the colonies their money, which created unemployment and dissatisfaction. The inability of the colonists to get power to issue their own money permanently out of the hands of George III and the international bankers was the prime reason for the Revolutionary War."

This is a remarkable quote from one of America's founding fathers. School kids are taught the story of the Boston Tea Party and the rallying cry for the American Revolution was taxation without representation; true but incomplete. There never would have been a problem with taxation without the loss of control of the Colonial currency. The "little tax on tea" was nothing compared to the usury of the Bank of England. Inflation and the debasement of currency destroy economies; taxation can slow an economy but it can also provide necessary governmental services. Modern day tax protesters don't see the big picture. They will never control taxation without first controlling the currency. The loss of control of a currency is the gaping, oozing wound; taxation is the salt on the wound.

"Let me issue and control a nation's money and I care not who writes the laws." - Mayer Amschel Rothschild, founder of the Rothschild international banking dynasty.

Many of the founding fathers and leading statesmen were pronounced in their opposition to central banking and usury and debt.

"History records that the money changers have used every form of abuse, intrigue, deceit and violent means possible, to maintain their control over governments, by controlling money and its issuance." – James Madison, on the First Central Bank. Madison was the fourth President of the United States and considered the Father of the Constitution. Two centuries later his words hold true.

"The banking system concentrates and places the power in the hands of those who control it. Never was an engine invented better calculated to place the destinies of the many in the hands of the few, or less favorable to that equality and independence which lies at the bottom of out free institutions." – John C. Calhoun, two time Vice President, Senator, and Secretary of State. Calhoun understood the power of banks to centralize power and concentrate wealth in the hands of oligarchs.

"I object to the continuance of this bank because its tendencies are dangerous and pernicious to the government and the people. It tends to aggravate the inequalities of fortunes; to make the rich richer, and the poor poorer; to multiply the nabobs and paupers, and to deepen and widen the gulf that separates Dives from Lazarus." – Thomas H. Benton, US Senator. The income gap and wealth disparity was a concern in the early days of the Republic and those gaps have now grown to extremes.

"If the American people ever allow private banks to control the issue of their currency, the banks and corporations that will grow up around them will deprive the people of all property until their children wake-up homeless on the continent their fathers conquered." - Thomas Jefferson: *"The Debate Over The Recharter Of The Bank Bill"*, 1809.

"And I sincerely believe with you, that banking establishments are more dangerous than standing armies; and that the principle of spending money to be paid by posterity, under the name of funding, is but swindling futurity on a large scale" – Thomas Jefferson in a letter to John Taylor, 1816.

We can't say the Founding Fathers didn't warn us.

The first bank of the United States was incorporated in 1781; it failed. The second official First Bank of the United States was incorporated in 1791; despite fierce opposition from several of the Founding Fathers, a charter was granted for twenty years.

When the charter expired in 1811, attempts to renew the charter were defeated. The bankers were persistent and in 1816 a new charter was granted, expiring in 1836. In 1832, President Andrew Jackson ordered funds removed from the Second Bank of the United States and held in safes. Nicholas Biddle, the head of the Second Bank and backed by the House of Rothschild, threatened to throw the country into a depression if the bank's charter was not renewed. There was a depression, but the charter was revoked by Jackson's veto. For almost thirty years the United States had no public debt.

"Events have satisfied my mind, and I think the minds of the American people, that the mischief and dangers which flow from a national bank far overbalance all its advantages." – Andrew Jackson, seventh President of US.

"Gentlemen, I have had men watching you for a long time and I am convinced that you have used the funds of the bank to speculate in the breadstuffs of the country. When you won, you divided the profits amongst you, and when you lost, you charged it to the bank. You tell me that if I take the deposits from the bank and annul its charter I shall ruin ten thousand families. That may be true, gentlemen, but that is your sin! Should I let you go on you will ruin fifty thousand families, and that would be my sin! You are a den of vipers and thieves. I have determined to rout you out, and by the Eternal God, I will rout you out!" – Andrew Jackson, speaking to bankers in the White House.

Jackson's battle against the bank was long and dangerous. There was an assassination attempt that failed. When Andrew Jackson was asked what he considered the greatest achievement of his career he answered without hesitation, "I killed the bank."

Indeed, a battle for control of money continued. Absent a central bank, the fractional reserve system migrated to state chartered banks. In times of peace there was little need for a central bank; costs could be controlled, but wars are expensive. Wars require huge expenditures, and a central bank can finance those expenditures by producing money out of thin air and then charging interest on the debt. Bankers and war go hand in hand through history; from the Venetians to William and Mary, to the Napoleonic Wars, to the American Revolution, to the Civil War.

Abraham Lincoln addressed the problem of financing the Civil War, and how little control government actually had over the bankers, whom he described as his "greatest foe". Faced with the bankers' excessive rates of up to 36% to finance the war, Lincoln opted to print script to pay soldiers. The script was printed with green ink on the back to differentiate it from earlier notes, and was known as greenbacks. By 1863, Congress balked at printing more script and the bankers swooped in. The declaration to establish a central bank to issue debt passed as an emergency war measure. The National Bank Act, first adopted in 1863, provides for the establishment and regulation of national banks. For more than 100 years, that law was interpreted to require that even national banks can only charge interest at the rate allowed by the state in which its customer is located. The loan was confined to war debt and the time of payment was restricted to twenty years. Once debt is established it is difficult to break free. The war debt was extended, or re-funded, and charters were renewed. Bonds were no longer limited to covering war expenses, but were issued in times of peace.

Lincoln's opposition to the central bank's financial control was well documented: "Right after the Civil War there was considerable talk about reviving Lincoln's brief experiment with the Constitutional monetary system. Had not the European money-trust intervened, it would have no doubt become an established institution." - W. Cleon Skousen, author.

The Civil War had raised the national debt 25 times over. Lincoln's second term campaign included promises to repeal the central bank charter and return to the gold standard. Of course, Lincoln was assassinated less than 2 months after his re-election.

The United States suffered through a terrible Depression in the 1870's as the bankers contracted money supply. When James Garfield was elected president in 1980, he knew the economy was a top priority and he also knew that he would not be in control of the economy. Garfield geared up for a Jacksonian fight against the central bank: "Whosoever controls the volume of money in any country is absolute master of all industry and commerce... And when you realise that the entire system is very easily controlled, one way or another, by a few powerful men at the top, you will not have to be told how periods of inflation and depression originate." The fight never got started, as Garfield was assassinated shortly after his inauguration.

While wars are expensive and profitable for financiers, boom and bust cycles can also be profitable; first the prices get pushed higher – all financed – and then the banks can contract the money supply and acquire assets on the cheap: "On Sept 1st, 1894, we will not renew our loans under any consideration. On Sept 1st we will demand our money. We will foreclose and become mortgagees in possession. We can take two-thirds of the farms west of the Mississippi, and thousands of them east of the Mississippi as well, at our own price... Then the farmers will become tenants as in

England..." – 1891, American Bankers Association, as printed in the Congressional Record of April 29, 1913.

If this tactic seems familiar, it is because it was repeated 117 years later.

The Panic of 1907 was fed by "bucket shops," where people made bets on a security, commodity or whatever without actually buying or selling it. Unlike their customers, the shops actually owned blocks of stock. If customers were betting that a stock would go up, the shops would sell it and the price would plunge; if bettors were bearish, the shops would buy. In this way, they cleaned out their customers. New York State outlawed bucket shops in 1909, and other states followed suit. It is mentioned here because this is yet another scheme that bankers would resurrect some 90 years later, under the new name "derivatives".

It was Woodrow Wilson who finally conceded to the demands for a central bank by signing the Federal Reserve Act into law in 1913, a maneuver that effectively passed control of the American monetary system to private interests, the Federal Reserve Bank. The Federal Reserve Bank that currently issues the currency of the United States of America is a private institution whose shareholders are the member banks. The United States of America does not issue its own currency.

President Wilson broke his campaign promises and signed into law the Federal Reserve Act, with some remorse: "I am a most unhappy man. I have unwittingly ruined my country. A great industrial nation is controlled by its system of credit. Our system of credit is concentrated. The growth of the nation therefore, and all our activities, are in the hands of a few men. We have come to be one of the worst ruled, one of the most completely controlled and dominated Governments in the civilized world. No longer a Government by free opinion, no longer a Government by conviction and the vote of the majority, but a Government by the opinion and duress of a small group of dominant men."

And so, with the creation of the Federal Reserve banking system in the United States, usury became the accepted and normal condition. The bankers could now create *and* lend money. They could appropriate interest and capital. The power of usury now came, not just from charging interest, but creating new claims and appropriating those claims. The bank could create money out of thin air and charge interest: "The study of money, above all other fields in economics, is one in which complexity is used to disguise truth or to evade truth, not to reveal it. The process by which banks create money is so simple the mind is repelled. With something so important, a deeper mystery seems only decent." - John Kenneth Galbraith, former professor of economics at Harvard, writing in *"Money: Whence it came, where it went"*.

Most people were not even aware of the change that was coming: "It is well enough that people of the nation do not understand our banking and money system, for if they did, I believe there would be a revolution before tomorrow morning." Henry Ford, founder of the Ford Motor Company.

Chapter 5

The Great Depression – The Only Thing We Have to Fear is … Bankers

The bankers could create money and they could also create booms and busts, which were very profitable. Debt inevitably leads to booms and busts. The economy expands when money is borrowed and put into circulation. The economy contracts when the debt must be repaid. Bankers could finance wars, which were also profitable. Wars destroy things, which have to be replaced; the purchase price is financed by debt. Central banking failed to bring economic stability. The thirty years that followed the creation of the Fed marked some of the most challenging times in America's history: World War I, the Panic of 1920, the Great Depression, and World War II.

Immediately after World War I, the Federal Reserve debased the dollar to help rebuild the British economy. In order to lower the value of the dollar and raise the value of the pound, the Fed embarked on purposeful monetary expansion. Money supply expanded from $12 billion in 1914 to $26 billion in 1929. The result of monetary expansion was the Roaring Twenties, a huge stock market boom, and equities that kept being bid higher as cheap money poured into the economy. The challenge for the bankers was to keep the stock market flying high.

The banks could lend based upon fractional reserves but they still faced pesky state usury laws which limited the amount of interest they could charge. Investment banking added a new dimension to usury – leverage. And the perfect vehicle for investment banking was the Investment Trust. An Investment Trust could raise cash by selling its own paper. For example, the Investment Trust G could raise $150 million worth of cash, by issuing $150 million of its own paper: $50 million of its own bonds, $50 million of its own preferred stock, and $50 million of its own common stock. After the sale of its own instruments, Investment Trust G uses the $150 million in cash to buy the common stock of other companies, such as AT&T, Ford, GM, and US Steel. These stocks became Investment Trust G's assets.

In the 1920's, the fractional reserve banking system had inflated the money supply and much of the inflated money went to the stock market. Assume all common stocks rise, on average, by 50% in value. Then, the assets that Investment Trust G owns, which were worth $150 million, would now be worth $225 million. If the value of Investment Trust G's *assets* are worth $225 million, then the value of the *paper* that Investment Trust has issued---its bonds, preferred stock, and common stock--should reflect this increase, by also being worth $225 million; bonds worth $75 million, preferred stock worth $75 million, and common stock worth $75 million.

But the bonds and preferreds only paid interest and dividends, and the only paper issued by Investment Trust that could rise in value is the common stock. Since the total value of Investment Trust G was now worth $225 million, then the value of common stock issued by Investment Trust G increased in value from $50 million before, to $125 million now.

The value of the assets--the common stock of other companies--that Investment Trust G owned, increased in value by 50%; but the value of Investment Trust G's own common stock increased in value by 150% (from $50 million to $125 million), that is, at a rate three times greater than the common stock of other companies that Investment Trust G owns. That's leverage. In this example, the ratio of leverage is 3:1, between the increase in the value of common stock, and its production of a threefold increase in the value of Investment Trust common stock.

But why stop there: You could theoretically set up another Investment Trust, let's call it Investment Trust S, which would buy up and hold the common stock of Investment Trust G. Investment Trust S would issue bonds, preferred stock, and common stock; and Investment Trust S would buy the common stock of Investment Trust G. If the leverage of Investment Trust G to the common stocks it held was 3, and the leverage of Investment Trust S to Investment Trust G was 3, then the leverage of Investment Trust S to the common stock in the portfolio of Investment Trust G was 9:1.

This is a hypothetical example, but it is based upon the very real formula of the Goldman Sachs Trading Company, and its subsidiaries Shenandoah Inc. and BlueRidge Inc. Of course, the Goldman Sachs Trading Company did not produce anything, they did not manufacture any product, and they did not provide any particular service beyond moving paper around. And Goldman Sachs was not unique; many banks were speculating in the market, pushing depositors to become investors in their schemes. Everyday investors borrowed money, on margin, to invest in the stock market, which became artificially inflated. Leverage resulted in the Roaring Twenties, a bubble economy.

Eventually the Ponzi Scheme collapsed. There were certainly other causes of the Great Depression, but the new turbocharged leverage was definitely a big contributor. This was merely another form of usury; taking money from depositors to gamble in stocks and increasing the bet through leverage. The gamble failed in 1929.

Unemployment climbed to 25% and millions of Americans lost their homes to foreclosure. Shantytowns called Hoovervilles, named after President Hoover, sprang up across the country, the most notable in New York's Central Park. In 1932, the Bonus Army demanded immediate payment of their Service Certificates. Throughout American history, soldiers had received bonuses for their service, typically cash plus acreage; World War I vets only received a $60 cash bonus. The American Legion fought for veterans' bonuses, and in 1924 the government issued Service Certificates with a 20 year maturity. Faced with the hardships of the Depression, more than 40,000 World War I veterans marched on the Capitol, built a Hooverville along the Anacostia River, and demanded immediate payment of their Service Certificates.

Military troops led by General Douglas MacArthur and General George Patton, along with local police, attacked the veterans with fixed bayonets and gas; the US Army attacked its own veterans. Hundreds of veterans were injured and several were killed. The veterans marched again the next year, but it was not until 1936 that the bonuses were finally paid. The determination of the Bonus Army surely affected the 1944 decision to create the GI Bill of Rights.

The nation's banking system had collapsed by the time Franklin Roosevelt was inaugurated. Over 11,000 banks had failed. President Roosevelt's first words were to calm a nervous country, "The only thing we have to fear is fear itself"; that is the memorable line, but it was followed by strong condemnation of the true culprits:

"Plenty is at our doorstep, but a generous use of it languishes in the very sight of the supply. Primarily this is because rulers of the exchange of mankind's goods have failed through their own stubbornness and their own incompetence, have admitted their failure, and have abdicated. Practices of the unscrupulous money changers stand indicted in the court of public opinion, rejected by the hearts and minds of men.

"True they have tried, but their efforts have been cast in the pattern of an outworn tradition. Faced by failure of credit they have proposed only the lending of more money. Stripped of the lure of profit by which to induce our people to follow their false leadership, they have resorted to exhortations, pleading tearfully for restored confidence. They know only the rules of a generation of self-seekers. They have no vision, and when there is no vision the people perish.

"The money changers have fled from their high seats in the temple of our civilization. We may now restore that temple to the ancient truths."

The next day FDR declared a banking holiday, closing the doors of the banks. Eight days later he allowed "the most sound" banks to reopen.

Congressional hearings showed that the presumed leaders of American enterprise, the bankers and brokers, were guilty of disreputable and dishonest dealings and gross misuses of the public's trust, literally buying control of politicians. The hearings started in 1932 and they uncovered plenty of abuses. JP Morgan maintained a "preferred list" of clients that would get special deals, huge discounts on stock purchases that could then be flipped for a quick profit. Among the clients on the "preferred list": former President Calvin Coolidge, Supreme Court Justice Owen J. Roberts, former head of the Democratic Party John Raskob, and diplomat Norman Davis. The bankers had truly bribed their way into government.

J.P. Morgan, Jr., the son of the founder of the banking empire, testified that he had not paid any income taxes in 1930, 1931, and 1932; and dozens of multi-millionaire partners in JP Morgan had also not paid taxes. The revelation that the wealthiest Americans were not paying income tax must be juxtaposed against the desperate demands of the Bonus Army.

The hearings of 1932 ultimately led to reforms: "The Glass-Steagall Act was enacted to remedy the speculative abuses that infected commercial banking prior to the collapse of the stock market and the financial panic of 1929-1933. Many banks, especially national banks, not only invested heavily in speculative securities but entered the business of investment banking in the traditional sense of the term by buying original issues for public resale. Apart from the special problems confined to affiliation three well-defined evils were found to flow from the combination of investment and commercial banking." – *Investment Company Institute v. Camp.*

The three evils of the combined investment/commercial banks were: 1) banks were investing their own assets in securities with consequent risk to commercial and savings deposits; 2) loans were made in order to shore up the price of securities or the financial position of companies in which a bank had invested its own assets; 3) and commercial banks' financial interest in the ownership, price, or distribution of securities inevitably tempted bank officials to press their banking customers into investing in securities which the bank itself was under pressure to sell because of its own stake in the transaction.

The Glass-Steagall Act was one of the pillars of banking law since its passage in 1933. Glass-Steagall built a wall between commercial banking and investment banking. The law kept commercial banks that accept deposits from doing business on Wall Street as investment banks that issue and trade securities, and vice versa. There are actually two Glass Steagall measures. The first was the Glass-Steagall Act of 1932, a bookkeeping provision that allowed the Treasury to balance its account. And what is commonly known today as the Glass-Steagall law is actually the Bank Act of 1933, containing the provision erecting a wall between the banking and securities businesses. The Glass-Steagall Act also permitted Reserve Banks to make loans to member banks on any security the Reserve Banks consider satisfactory, and in unusual circumstances even to make loans to nonbank borrowers. It also established the Federal Deposit Insurance Corporation, or FDIC, to insure bank clients' deposits. The bankers had so thoroughly abused depositors' confidence that insured accounts were the only way to lure depositors back to banks, and to avert a run on the banks; even then millions of Americans would never trust the banks again.

The Bank Act of 1933 also included: the Truth in Securities Act and the Securities Exchange Act. The Truth in Securities Act required full disclosure in the issue of new securities to the public. Heavy penalties would be levied for failure to give full and accurate information about securities to the government. The Securities Exchange Act created the Securities and Exchange Commission, SEC, to regulate and oversee the securities markets. Certain manipulative practices, such as washed sales (selling stock, claiming a loss for tax purposes, and then buying it back in less than 30 days – or the mere pretence of a sale) and matched orders (creating pools to buy shares outside the exchanges, limiting supply and pushing prices higher), were prohibited. Insider trading was eliminated, or at least criminalized.

In April of 1933, President Roosevelt signed an order requiring citizens to turn in their gold for $20.67 per ounce. A few people surrendered their gold. The idea was to stop a "run" on the government by people demanding gold for their paper dollars; because of fractional reserve banking there never was enough gold to match the paper dollars that had been printed. The price of gold from the treasury was then raised to $35 per ounce, effectively increasing the money supply by 59%, and posting a nice profit for the Treasury.

The Bank Act of 1933 would remain largely intact until the Depository Institutions Act of 1980, and it was obliterated in 1999 by the Gramm-Leach-Bliley Act. Not surprisingly, many of the abuses of the 1920's would be revisited after these regulations were taken away.

FDR would continue to attack the bankers throughout most of his administration: "The real truth of the matter is, as you and I know, that a financial element in the larger centers has owned the

Government ever since the days of Andrew Jackson — and I am not wholly excepting the Administration of W. W. The country is going through a repetition of Jackson's fight with the Bank of the United States — only on a far bigger and broader basis."

The banking reforms continued. The Banking Act of 1935 restructured the Federal Reserve System, and introduced the basic structure that exists today. The Treasury Secretary and Comptroller of the Currency no longer serve on the Board. The Commodities Exchange Act of 1936 set regulations for trading futures options and commodities on registered and regulated exchanges. The Act provided federal regulation of all commodities and futures trading activities and required all futures and commodity options to be traded on organized exchanges.

FDR remained vigilant against the abuses of the bankers through his first two terms: "We have begun to bring private autocratic powers into their proper subordination to the public's government. The legend that they were invincible--above and beyond the processes of a democracy--has been shattered. They have been challenged and beaten." Also: "The test of our progress is not whether we add more to the abundance of those who have much; it is whether we provide enough for those who have too little."

Many people now believe that all government is bad. Perhaps it has taken a turn for the worse, but how can a democratically elected government be bad when it serves the will of the People? Bankers and

Corporatist use this demonization to combat the "one person – one vote" rule. If you ask citizens about the quality of our military, police, or NASA everyone says they are the best in the world. Our state run university system attracts the brightest minds from all over the world. Senior citizens, by an overwhelming majority think that Medicare works great for them. All are government programs. Control is in the hands of the bankers and Corporatists who want the People to fight government so they keep power.

The Depression-era bankers may have taken a beating, but they rose like vampires to suck profits in World War II. The national debt increased six fold. The national debt in 1946, the year after the war ended, was 128 per cent of gross national product. While soldiers paid the ultimate price, the financiers were collecting hefty premiums on the debt. The most despicable act of treason is war profiteering. Blood, severed limbs, and life itself must never be sacrificed for profit. The fight for freedom does not include the perverse freedom to profit from patriots' blood.

Since the end of World War II, the US dollar enjoyed a unique and dominant position in international trade. In the summer of 1944, before the war ended, 44 nations sent delegates to a conference in Bretton Woods, New Hampshire, and they created a system for exchanging one currency against another. It also led to the creation of the International Monetary Fund (IMF) and the International Bank for Reconstruction and Development, now known as the World Bank. The IMF was designed to monitor exchange rates and lend reserve currencies to nations with trade deficits. The IBRD/World Bank was designed to provide underdeveloped nations with needed capital — although each institution's role has changed over time. The member states agreed to fix their exchange rates by tying their currencies to the US dollar, and the dollar was fixed to gold at $35 per ounce. Central banks were given the job of maintaining fixed exchange rates between their currencies and the dollar. They did this by intervening in foreign exchange markets. If a country's currency was too high relative to the dollar, its central bank would sell its currency in exchange for dollars, driving down the value of its currency. Conversely, if the value of a country's money was too low, the country would buy its own currency, pushing the price up. The United States became the money manager for the world. The theory was that the Bretton Woods system would promote stability; the reality was quite different.

The dollar was king, but US foreign policy sometimes imposed onerous restrictions on the use of the dollar as a global reserve currency. After 1965, US behavior became increasingly destabilizing, mostly as a result of increased government spending on social programs at home and an escalating war in Vietnam. America's economy began to overheat and inflation began to gain momentum, causing deficits to widen. Foreign governments realized the US was printing money, which was theoretically, backed by gold. The flood of dollars caused demand for gold to surge. Foreign governments (especially France) began cashing in the paper dollars for gold. Of course, the US didn't have enough gold to back its dollars.

In 1971, President Richard Nixon signed the Smithsonian Agreement, which devalued the dollar in its relation to gold. It would now take $38 dollars to buy an ounce of gold, up from $35; Nixon then cut the connection between the dollar and gold. Inflation increased. In 1973, Nixon again devalued the dollar to $42.22 per ounce of gold, nearly 20% devaluation in two years. Confidence in the dollar was dashed. President Ford would later lift restrictions on gold ownership and gold prices jumped dramatically. Inflation skyrocketed.

By 1978, inflation had made lending unprofitable. The prime rate was 11.75%, higher than most states' usury limits; by 1980, the prime rate topped out at 20%, essentially matching the devaluation of the dollar in 1971. And those pesky state laws that limit usury? They are still on the books in several states. The basic idea behind the usury laws was to avoid excessive interest rates. Low interest rates limit inflation, but the usury laws could not stop inflation when the dollar had been devalued.

Slowly but surely, the banks chipped away at the state usury laws. Each state had its own limits, a balancing act between attracting lenders and protecting its citizens. Generally, state usury laws placed maximum caps between 6% to about 18% on loans, but the laws became riddled with holes; exemptions for business loans, car loans, and mail-order loans – but no exemptions for an individual making a loan to another individual. To charge more than the legal limit was a crime. The criminals were known as loan sharks.

Before we get to the monumental changes in usury laws, we need to go back to 1950, when Frank X. McNamara, head of the Hamilton Credit Corp. went to dinner with Albert Bloomingdale, heir to the department stores. Charge cards came into use around 1914, when Western Union and various department stores, hotels, and oil companies began using them. These early cards could be used to purchase the issuer's goods and services only, and balances had to be paid in full each month. McNamara and Bloomingdale discussed a client of Hamilton Credit who had allowed neighbors to borrow his store charge cards to make purchases at local stores. The man charged his neighbors interest on the purchases but when the neighbors became delinquent on their payments, the man was forced to ask Hamilton Credit for a loan. Meanwhile, McNamara forgot his wallet and he had to call his wife to bring him cash to pay for the meal. The idea for the Diners' Club was hatched.

Diners' Club, the first credit card, was initially accepted by 14 restaurants in the New York area. The Diners Club was going to be a middleman. Instead of individual companies offering credit to their own customers, the Diners Club offered credit to individuals from many companies and then billed the customers and paid the companies, relieving the companies from collection duties. The restaurants were charged 7 percent and the card holder paid an annual fee of $3. By the end of the first year, 20,000 customers were using the Diners' Club card.

In 1958, American Express and BankAmeriCard (which later became Visa) got into the act. Bank of America issued the first BankAmeriCard by mass mailing 60,000 cards to the residents of Fresno, California. BankAmeriCard was the first credit card based on a revolving line of credit. The bank was swamped by massive defaults on the cards. In 1966, a group of Midwestern banks attempted another mass mailing of five million cards. The cards were mailed indiscriminately and this was probably the first time, but not the last, that a dog was issued a credit card. Cards were stolen from the mail and fraud was rampant. Congressional hearings on the "Chicago Debacle" included calls to outlaw credit cards, but the cards were a successful way for banks to lure new customers even if the credit card unit didn't pull in big profits, and for the consumer the lure was irresistible. The credit card companies linked a nationwide network of merchants and banks under the brands of Visa and MasterCard. The debt habit was diligently cultivated and encouraged. By 1978, over 100 million cards had been issued.

The banks had plenty of credit card customers but they couldn't make profits in an inflationary economy that capped usury. For the credit card companies, it was no longer a matter of chipping away at usury limits; they began pounding the legal limits with a sledgehammer.

Section 2 – The Road to Financial Armageddon

Chapter 6

1978 – The Turning Point, Usury Foisted on America

The Supreme Court changed everything in 1978 with its ruling on *Marquette National Bank of Minneapolis v. First of Omaha Service Corp.* First of Omaha was a national banking association chartered as Omaha Bank, based in Nebraska, where usury was capped at 18 percent. Omaha Bank enrolled in the BankAmeriCard system and solicited business in Minnesota.

Marquette was a national banking association chartered in Minnesota and also enrolled in the BankAmeriCard system. Minnesota allowed usury rates up to 9 percent.

Omaha Bank charged its BankAmeriCard customers in Minnesota at the 18 percent rate allowed in Nebraska.

The Court held in *Marquette* that the National Bank Act of 1863 authorizes a national banking association "to charge on any loan" interest at the rate allowed by the laws of the State "where the bank is located". Justice William Brennan defended his decision: "Minnesota residents were always free to visit Nebraska and receive loans in that state." It hadn't been suggested that Minnesota's laws would apply in that instance. Therefore, Minnesota's usury laws shouldn't be applied just because "the convenience of modern mail" allowed Minnesotans to get credit without having to visit Nebraska. The *Marquette* decision applied to all types of consumer loans, but it had the greatest consequences for the credit card industry.

The Supreme Court decision drew little attention at the time. It didn't take long for banks to connect the dots. If a bank could locate in a state with high, or no, usury limits they could export the high rates to any state in the country; if a bank could get one state to wipe out its usury laws that would effectively wipe out the usury laws in all states.

Like many states in 1980, South Dakota was suffering economically. Citibank attacked with the efficiency of a lion going after a lame lamb. The South Dakota legislature quickly passed laws that repealed the state's usury limits; Citibank actually drafted the legislation. In return, Citibank moved its credit card headquarters and jobs to Rapid City, South Dakota. Wells Fargo also moved its credit card headquarters to South Dakota. South Dakota's delusions of becoming Wall Street on the frozen plains were soon dashed. One year later Delaware passed legislation that wiped out its usury laws, and more banks rushed to move their operations.

In 1980, President Jimmy Carter imposed a freeze on soliciting new credit card accounts in an effort to tame inflation. The freeze only lasted a few months but in that time the credit card companies added a new way to fleece customers, the annual fee. Credit card companies had seen profits drop from 4% of outstanding balances in 1977 to losses of 1% in 1979, but profits were just around the corner. Carter gave another, unintended gift to the banks: the Depository Institutions Deregulation and Monetary Control Act (DIDMCA) of 1980.

DIDMCA put banks under the wing of the Federal Reserve, allowed banks to merge, allowed credit unions and savings and loans to offer checking accounts, and raised the limits on FDIC insurance from $40,000 per account to $100,000 per account. President Carter, in signing the Act, also claimed DIDMCA would allow small savers to earn higher returns on their savings accounts by lifting interest rate ceilings – but that was a two-edged sword; DICMCA lifted interest rates on what banks could pay depositors *and* what they could charge borrowers. DIDMCA exempted federally chartered savings banks, installment plan sellers, and chartered loan companies from state usury limits. The banks could now charge whatever they wanted.

Over 4,000 years of laws that had protected people from the injustices of usury were, essentially, destroyed.

Over the past three decades there has been a steady stream of legislation that has emboldened the usurers and buried the borrowers.

Home mortgage interest rates were still capped by usury laws; the Alternative Mortgage Transaction Parity Act (AMTPA) of 1982 killed that protection. If the banks couldn't eliminate the usury limits on mortgages they could still circumvent the laws with smoke and mirrors. AMTPA preempted state laws that restricted banks from making any mortgage except conventional fixed rate mortgages. AMTPA allowed adjustable rate mortgages, balloon payment mortgages, and interest only mortgages; a wide range of exotic lending vehicles that were largely incomprehensible for most borrowers. The law allowed lenders to make loans with terms that obscure the total cost of a loan. This law was a major contributor to predatory and subprime loans in the housing bubble of the early 2000s.

The Interstate Banking Act of 1994 served to eliminate restrictions on interstate banking, opening the door for banks to merge, without concern for state charters, and further consolidating the power of the big banks.

In 1996, Citibank's South Dakota operations would figure in a related Supreme Court case, *Smiley v. Citibank*. This time, state regulations on the late fees charged by credit-card issuers were challenged, and again the court ruled unanimously that they were also pre-empted by the National Banking Act, as interpreted by the Comptroller of Currency.

In 1998, Citibank merged with Travelers. The new company, called Citigroup, combined a commercial bank holding company with an insurance company; a one stop shop for banking (Citibank), insurance (Travelers), and investing (Smith Barney, Primerica, Citifinancial). At the time it was the largest merger in history and created a financial behemoth with operations in 100 countries. It was also illegal, based upon the Glass-Steagall Act of 1933.

Citigroup and other bankers set out to change the law. Their lobbying efforts cost $300 million dollars and produced fast results.

Senator Phil Gramm, who received more than $4.6 million from Finance, Insurance and Real Estate campaign donations, led the assault. Gramm would eventually become a consultant for the Swiss Bank, UBS. Treasury Secretary Robert Rubin, a former partner at Goldman Sachs and soon to be Director of Citigroup, also championed the repeal of Glass-Steagall.

In 2009, John Reed, the Co-founder of Citigroup, came to regret the repeal of Glass-Steagall. "I would compartmentalize the (banking) industry for the same reason you compartmentalize ships," Reed said. "If you have a leak, the leak doesn't spread and sink the whole vessel. So generally speaking you'd have consumer banking separate from trading bonds and equity." Ten years after his treasonous deal, Reed tried to justify his greed, "When you're running a company, you do what you think is right for the stockholders. Right now I'm looking at this as a citizen." Apparently, Citigroup management must renounce citizenship as a requisite for employment.

The Gramm-Leach-Bliley Act of 1999, also known as the Financial Service Modernization Act of 1999, finally killed the Glass-Steagall Act of 1933. Other financial mergers followed on the heels of Citigroup. The wall between commercial banks and investment banks was torn down. Commercial banks were supposed to accept customer's deposits and protect those deposits. Investment banks organized sales of bonds and equities, which can be a risky business. It would not take long for the financial behemoths to start making reckless bets with depositors' money.

Now that banks were legally allowed to gamble with depositors' money, the next step was to increase the odds; the tool was leverage, and that meant killing off a few more laws.

The Commodity Futures Modernization Act of 2000 was written with the help of financial industry lobbyists and cosponsored by Senators Richard Lugar and Phil Gramm. The Act was tacked onto thousands of pages of a budget bill in the final hours before a vote; it is doubtful that any legislators read the complete Act before voting. The Act removed regulation on newfangled financial products called swaps and derivatives. According to Gramm, the act would "protect financial institutions from overregulation" and "position our financial services industries to be world leaders into the new century." What it did was to turn banks into a modern version of the bucket shops that caused the Panic of 1907. Like the old bucket shops, banks were now allowed to place private bets, called derivatives, on underlying assets (such as commodities, securities, or anything they wanted to bet on). The bets were private and did not fall under the regulation of public exchanges.

Credit Default Swaps, CDS, are derivatives that are essentially insurance policies covering the losses on securities in the event of a default; financial institutions buy them to protect themselves if an investment they hold goes south. It's like bookies trading bets, with banks and hedge funds gambling on whether an investment, (a portfolio of bonds, mortgages, or almost any other type of security) will succeed or fail.

CDS is not typical insurance; it is almost completely unregulated; an investor can purchase a CDS contract/insurance policy even though they have no insurable interest in the security that is being insured. We do not allow strangers to buy life insurance policies against strangers because of the fear that the investor will kill off the insured to collect. We do not allow doctors to purchase life insurance policies on their patient's lives without the patient's knowledge, and then be in charge of making life and death decisions for the patient's treatment. We all recognize that it is reckless and foolhardy to subject that doctor/patient trust to excessive temptation. CDS offered a clear incentive for investors to hope for, or possibly even take action to force defaults.

The CDS market quickly grew to more than $60 trillion dollars, nearly four times the size of the entire US stock market and four times the gross domestic product; and because it was unregulated, no one made sure the banks and hedge funds and insurance companies that sold the CDS/insurance had the assets to cover the losses they guaranteed. Even a bookie knows he can't win every bet.

Another step in protecting the financial behemoths from overregulation was a 2004 decision by the SEC to improve the odds on their fractional reserves, and allow banks to leverage to the hilt. Banks had been required to keep reserves of money against loans. The old rule was 12:1, meaning banks could loan $12 dollars for every $1 dollar held in reserve. The new ratio was changed to 33:1, meaning banks could loan $33 dollars for every $1 held in reserve. A 3% loss could now wipe out reserves.

The casino banks were ready for business. Of course, one of the problems with running a casino is that your customers tend to go broke. And the banks had rigged the game to ensure their customers would go broke: credit cards companies could now charge usurious rates of 29% or more, and exotic mortgages could suddenly balloon to rates of 18% or more. The Credit Default Swaps were insurance designed to pay off when loans went bad. Instead of holding cash reserves for bad loans, the banks could now hold derivatives to act like reserves.

The entire economy had shifted from production to consumption (more on this later in the book). Following September 11, 2001 President George W. Bush reminded Americans that it was their patriotic duty to go to the mall and shop or "go down to Disneyland". The Federal Reserve rushed to flood the banks with money. Much of the shopping was paid for with plastic, and the ball and chain just got tighter and heavier.

Bankruptcy had always been a method for people to wipe their debts clean and get a fresh start. The idea of bankruptcy goes back to a biblical concept of Jubilee. The seventh day is a day of rest, the Sabbath; extending that idea, every seventh year was a Sabbatic year (Deut. 15:1), a year of rest, a year in which crops were not planted in the fields and all debt was suspended for the year. Every 49th year (seven years times seven) was a year of Jubilee in which all debts were cancelled; every last penny of debt wiped out and everybody gets a fresh start. Jubilee was considered an expression of God's mercy and forgiveness. Bankers' compassion is less than God-like.

The banks had a strategy to deal with customers who went broke; rather than stop lending to customers in financial trouble they decided to restrict the right to file for bankruptcy. The customers might never be able to pay their bills, but the bills would never disappear; in fact, the debt would grow larger as late fees and penalties were tacked on, and interest rates could be jacked sky high. The bankers had pushed this idea for years. In 2005, the banking industry drafted a new bankruptcy law, they mounted a $60 million dollar campaign and President Bush signed the Bankruptcy Reform Act, which could have been called the Debt Slave Act, which made it much tougher for people to get a fresh start. One of the provisions of the bill made sure child support payments would no longer take precedence over all credit card debt. The bankers had literally figured out how to take candy from a baby.

The firewalls that prevented conflicts of interest were torn down; the line between investing and speculation was erased; the escape exits were blocked. And they still wanted more.

Chapter 7

A Bubble World – Bankers and the Casino Mentality: Gambling With Your Money

Financial derivatives now account for 12 times the global GDP – more than $600 trillion dollars; for perspective, the global GDP for the entire history of the world prior to the year 2000 is estimated at less than $300 trillion dollars. Banks, insurance companies, hedge funds, private equity clients, sovereign funds, and even governments are leveraged at such high multiples it would make a chronic gambler blush. The amounts held in derivatives do not represent actual production, just the usurious gains. Bankers had built a new model for usury. In the past, usury was the gain on a loan – it represented interest and/or fees. The new version of usury allowed the bankers to create money out of thin air, and take their cut – in addition to interest and fees. The artificially created money did not represent a store of value or any other representation of production. The bankers added fees for risk. The bankers had not produced hundred of trillions of dollars worth of goods and services. They were gambling and calling it risk control or hedging, and thanks to deregulation, the chips they used were actual dollars.

Speculative investing has a long and dismal history; and all investing has risk. You can go back over the centuries and find examples of bankers manipulating prices, tucking away profits and passing losses to the masses; booms and busts, whether it was the Tulip Mania, the South Seas Trading Company, the California Gold Rush, or Wall Street in 1929.

More recent history (1980s) brought us the Leveraged Buy-out Boom, and the Savings and Loan Crisis. In the late 1980's, hundreds of insolvent S&Ls were still growing rapidly, just before the collapse. One of the most notorious S&L's was Lincoln Savings; its CEO, Charles Keating, was accused of buying undue influence with at least five politicians, known as the Keating Five. The money flowed like wine. Dealmakers structured junk bond debt to buy out companies that had previously managed to grow and prosper without massive debt. One of the more intriguing deals from the LBO Boom was the case of the largest drugstore chain in the country, Revco. Revco also became the largest leveraged buy-out to fail, insolvent on the day the deal closed. The buy-out was financed by junk bonds, and the debt burden left no margin for error; the purchasers of those bonds were supposedly sophisticated investors. The investment bankers destroyed the largest drug store in the country, but they still collected $80 million for their efforts.

President Reagan appointed Alan Greenspan as Chairman of the Federal Reserve. Greenspan oversaw several bubbles and crashes: the Crash of 87, the S&L Crisis, the dot.com bubble, the LTCM Collapse, Y2K, 9/11, and the housing bubble. The Federal Reserve controls the flow of money and they also serve as regulators.

Greenspan espoused a laissez faire approach to regulation, which is to say he didn't do his job as a regulator. He did let the money flow, starting with the Crash of 87. In times of turmoil, Greenspan's response was to throw money at the market. The market's response was to pick up the money, dust itself off and get back to work: crash, boom, crash, boom – but definitely not economic stability.

The 1990s were even more turbulent and irrationally exuberant. The technology revolution produced the world's first dot-com billionaire in 1995. And the more things changed the more they stayed the same. Just as the House of Morgan had created a "preferred list" of clients in the 1920s, investment bankers created a "hot list" for the dot.com bubble. There was a fever for the latest, newest technology and new companies appeared with regularity and those companies' shares were offered to the public in initial public offerings (IPOs). Even though many of the companies had no track record and no immediately sellable product or service, they were hot because they might represent the next big technology breakthrough. Share prices would sometimes double or triple in the first day of trading. The broad public could not get in on the "offered" price but special clientele could. The IPOs were frequently priced low in anticipation of a big opening day increase. Rather than capital going into the coffers of the new company, the money was soaked up by the brokerages and the hot list clients. IPO allocations from brokerages were awarded to corporate executives in the hope the executives would steer corporate finance work back to the brokerages. The practice became known as spinning. New technology also spawned dark pool trading - the anonymous trading of stocks away from the major exchanges. Dark pool trading is the computerized version of matched orders from the 1920s.

New technologies also led to computerized trading and quantitative analysis of asset classes and the creation of exotic new investment instruments. One of the earliest advocates of innovative financial vehicles tailored to investor needs was Long Term Capital Management. LTCM was a hedge fund formed by John Meriwether, the former head of bond trading at Salomon Brothers (which would eventually be swallowed up by Citigroup). Salomon Brothers was the largest bond trader and the top traders in the firm referred to themselves as "Big Swinging Dicks". Salomon became the first firm to issue MBS, mortgage backed securities. Meriwether recruited some brilliant mathematicians and traders for LTCM, including two Nobel Prize winners: Myron Scholes and Robert Merton. Only the brightest minds worked at LTCM and only the most sophisticated, high net worth ($1 million or more) investors were allowed to invest.

When LTCM collapsed in 1998, the highly leveraged hedge fund had become too big to fail and the Federal Reserve intervened to prevent a systemic failure of the global financial system. Fed Chairman Greenspan created a safety net for reckless speculation; it became known as the Greenspan Put. The concept of "too big to fail" also created a moral dilemma. Speculators could take enormous risks, threaten the global financial system, and if their bets paid off, they became very wealthy; if the bets failed, the losses would be covered by the Federal Reserve, or more accurately by taxpayers. The Greenspan Put socialized losses. Over the next decade speculation would grow exponentially, attracting capital from all segments of the economy and from all corners of the globe. Now that speculators had a safety net, they needed to find vehicles for their speculation.

Scholes, Merton, and Fischer Black were responsible for something called the Black-Scholes options pricing model. Options and futures are derivatives; they derive their value from an underlying asset, such as stocks or bonds or commodities or currencies. The Black-Scholes formula became a tool for pricing almost anything. Once a price is set, a portfolio can be configured to act like the underlying asset; think of it as reverse engineering. Collateralized Mortgage Obligations, CMOs, were pools of mortgages. Once the price and corresponding yield were set; mortgages were bundled into Mortgage Backed Securities (MBS) and then sliced into tranches, repackaged as CMOs and sold like high yield bonds. Of course, to achieve high yield required high risk mortgages to be sliced and diced in the mix. If you slice up a pool of mortgages, say one hundred times or more, it becomes very difficult to actually understand whether the mortgages, the underlying assets, are risky or safe.

Still other derivatives were created to insure banks against interest rate and currency fluctuations in the bank to bank market.

Credit insurance could be used to protect the investments in mortgage backed securities (MBS), which were then bundled into collateralized mortgage obligations (CMOs), packages of loans called Collateralized Loan Obligations (CLOs), and packages of debt called Collateralized Debt Obligations (CDOs). Everything from mortgages to car loans to credit card purchases to leveraged buy-outs could be insured. The ratings agencies that are supposed to analyze the risk and safety had an easy job; the securities were insured and thus safe. The credit insurance wasn't really insurance - it was a derivative; because once you can establish a price you can tailor a derivative to mimic the underlying asset – in this case the derivative looked like insurance. Unlike regular insurance, credit insurance, or credit default swaps, did not need reserves to protect against losses. They could now take bigger risks but the derivatives did not control risk, they just made the risks bigger. The bankers had created phony insurance to protect faux bonds.

Chapter 8

Setting the Stage for depression – The Bankers in Control: What Could Go Right?

Following the bursting of the tech bubble and in anticipation of Y2K, the Federal Reserve cut interest rates by 3 percent in a matter of months. After 9/11, the Fed cut rates all the way down to 1 percent, which was less than the rate of inflation, which is another way of saying the Fed was giving free money to bankers. Lower interest rates make mortgage payments cheaper, and demand for homes began to rise, sending prices up. Speculation was rampant. The normally slow and stodgy real estate market started trading with the frenzy of a meth freak on Red Bull. Flippers would buy property with no money down and sell the property within a week, pocketing tens of thousands of dollars, or more. In addition, millions of homeowners refinanced their existing mortgages, essentially turning their homes into ATMs and falling deeper in debt.

For the bankers it was boom time. As the industry ramped up, the quality of the mortgages went down; which really didn't matter to the lenders because they could take the good mortgages and mix them with the bad mortgages in Mortgage Backed Securities, which could then be sold, which meant the original lender no longer had skin in the game. In 2003, the Federal Reserve Chairman Greenspan said homeowners were losing "tens of thousands of dollars" by not taking one-year adjustable rate mortgages with a teaser rate of 3.25%. The main desire was to write as many loans as possible, predatory or not. Subprime lending jumped from $145 billion in 2001 to $625 billion in 2005. This incredible growth could only occur because the bankers could sell their predatory loans as Mortgage backed Securities (MBS) as fast as they could write them.

The banks no longer had to wait for a 30-year mortgage to pay off. The MBS was a way to sell future cash flow. A 30-year mortgage at about 7% interest would generate total payments approximately two-and-a-half times the purchase price of the property. Follow the money: A $500,000 note that was originated by Countrywide or ABC Mortgage Broker was sold to Wall Street Investment Bankers like Lehman Brothers or Goldman Sachs for about $600-650,000 as a mortgage backed security (MBS). Wall Street then transferred cash flow to a Mortgage Pool and issued $1.2-$1.5 million in CDO's – no need to wait 30 years. It has been widely alleged that Wall Street Bankers sold about $700,000 of CDO's from the Pool in this example to recapture their investment and have enough to pay themselves a nice bonus. The other $800,000 they didn't sell was transferred into Partnerships in the Cayman Islands and other tax havens, where they sat back and waited for these sub-prime loans to default and the Credit Default Swaps to pay them off – TAX FREE.

This was usury in the extreme. Usury is any gain on a loan. The banks were leveraging fractional reserves. The bankers started with $15,152 (of depositors' money, not their own), leveraged 33:1 to write the $500,000 mortgage, and through a series of securitizations turned that note into $1.5 million in derivatives, and then insured that derivative. They were selling the cash flow on the mortgages and then betting the mortgages would default. When the bankers robbed the future the real interest rate jumped to more than 1,000%.

Of course the bankers didn't keep the whole profit to themselves. The loot had to be split among the accomplices: realtors, appraisers, loan officers, loan originators, bond issuers, bond traders, accountants, mortgage servicers, CDS insurance traders, investors, Partnerships that acted as holders of mortgage backed securities in the

Cayman Islands and other tax havens, and the people who put their stamp of approval on the scam – the ratings agencies.

The ratings agencies (S&P, Fitch, Moody's – also known as *Nationally Recognized Statistical Ratings Organizations*) were supposed to analyze complex pools of debt, and the derivative securities created on top of the debt, and issue a grade that reflected the risk of the investment. The task was too complex for government regulators, and the ratings agencies became de facto regulators; if there was a problem it would show up in the rating, or so the argument went. The letter grade was not intended as a buy/sell recommendation, but that is what it became in day to day usage; a substitute for due diligence and a powerful sales tool. The high ratings assured investors, such as large corporations, hedge funds, and even pension funds, that they were getting a safe and sound investment. A high rated (triple A) security could be sold easily; while an F-rated or Junk rated security might never sell, even at a hefty discount. And the agencies sold AAA like a crack whore sells sex. The ratings agencies were paid by the bankers whose securities they rated, and the ratings agencies' fees were twice as big for subprime vs. prime backed portfolios. The bankers and the ratings agencies understood there was no point paying for a rating that could not be sold in the market place. The agencies worked hand in hand to assure a high grade. The bankers produced quantitative physicists to explain why subprime and Liar loans deserved AAA ratings. For the ratings agencies, it was like having a professor write your term paper.

One infamous email affirmed that understanding: ""We rate every deal," one S&P analyst wrote. "It could be structured by cows and we would rate it." With a strong rating, the derivatives could be insured against default with Credit Default Swaps (CDS), and if the derivatives were insured, they were deserving of their high rating; and since the derivatives were so highly rated, there was no need for the insurers to set aside reserves in the event of a default. The ratings agencies were alchemists capable of converting trash into cash.

Another email from a Standard & Poors employee sounds like an admission of guilt, "Let's hope we are all wealthy and retired by the time this house of cards falters."

In 2007, a Moody's employee wrote an email: "seems to me that we had blinders on and never questioned the information we were given. It is our job to think of the worst-case scenarios and model them." The e-mail continued: "Combined, these errors make us look either incompetent at credit analysis, or like we sold our soul to the devil for revenue." The agencies maintained high ratings even as the underlying securities slipped into default. It was not a matter of incompetence.

The bankers just needed to write mortgages, sell them, and get paid. When they ran out of the usual suspects – people with jobs, income, and savings – they took anybody who could fog a mirror. Countrywide, the largest mortgage lender, ran ads: "Bad Credit, No Income, No Problem." Lenders became predators; they misrepresented the terms of loans, they made loans without regard to consumers' ability to repay, they made loans with deceptive "teaser" rates that later ballooned astronomically, they packed loans with undisclosed charges and fees, and they even paid illegal kickbacks. The bankers argued that efforts to curb predatory lending would deny consumers access to credit, that it was discrimination.

One Citibank official said in a sworn affidavit that she regularly added extra fees to a home mortgage "if someone… was a minority." If the bankers could get away with predatory lending, they did, without regard to race, gender, credit worthiness, or income. The new discrimination was against anyone who didn't realize the banks were screwing them. The newly oppressed were call "subprime".

Chapter 9

Predatory Lending – Want a Piece of Candy?

Military families were targeted as customers during the boom in subprime lending because their frequent moves, overseas stints, and low pay meant they were more likely to have weak credit ratings. Turns out bankers consider soldiers to be subprime. It is true our troops are underpaid. The GI Bill didn't keep pace with inflation and when soldiers were forced to turn to bankers for help with housing their families, the bankers spit in their faces and slapped them with predatory loans. "We've never faced a situation like this, not in the

Vietnam War, World War II, or the Korean War, where so many military are in danger of losing their homes," said Paul Sullivan, executive director of Veterans for Common Sense, a Washington-based advocacy group started in 2002 by Iraq and Afghanistan War veterans. "No one asked them for their credit score when we asked them to fight for us."

When the initial teaser rates ran out, military families faced default rates four times the national average; towns around military bases became ground zero for foreclosures. Columbia, South Carolina, home to Fort Jackson, where the Army trains recruits for combat in Afghanistan and Iraq, saw foreclosure filings jump 8.3 times faster than the national average. Woodbridge, Virginia, next to the Marine Corps Base Quantico saw foreclosure filings 7 times greater than the national average. Foreclosure filings quadrupled in Norfolk, Virginia, home of the Navy's largest base. The Servicemembers' Civil Relief Act protects soldiers and sailors from losing homes for nonpayment of mortgages only while on active duty and for 90 days after they return home, but lenders aren't required to keep records of military status; the Act rarely stopped banks from harassing families. Troops returning from combat were faced with a new enemy that heaped stress upon stress.

The last time veterans lost homes to this extent was during the Great Depression when the Bonus Army marched on Washington and were turned back by our own troops wielding bayonets. Our treatment of our bravest warriors hasn't improved much in the past 80 years.

When America turns its back on veterans we abandon any claim to greatness; when we support bankers more than soldiers we have lost our moral compass.

In 2003, during the height of the predatory lending crisis, all 50 states' attorneys general brought litigation or entered into settlements with many subprime lenders that were engaged in predatory lending practices. Several state legislatures enacted laws aimed at curbing such practices. In 2004, the Office of the Comptroller of the Currency (OCC) invoked a clause from the 1863 National Bank Act to issue formal opinions pre-empting all state Anti-Predatory Lending laws, thereby rendering them inoperative. The OCC also created new rules that prevented states from enforcing any of their own consumer protection laws against national banks.

Conservatives have long argued that states' rights must be respected and that the Founding Fathers intended to create a republic with a limited centralized federal government. President Bush took the exact opposite position once he was in office, claiming that banks should "only be subject to federal laws regulating mortgage credit." Bush did nothing to protect homeowners and instead he aligned the federal government with the banks that were victimizing consumers. Predatory lending was given legal protection.

In 2008, several state attorneys general did file suit against Bank of America/Countrywide. Countrywide reached a settlement in all the cases, paid a few billion dollars and then B of A turned around and accepted several billion more in bailout money. Angelo Mozilo, the former head of Countrywide was implicated, but as of the time of this writing there has been no trial. California took the settlement money and went into the loan modification business, but it was too little, too late. Foreclosures continue to plague the Golden State like a wildfire in Santa Ana winds.

In 2009, the University of North Carolina published a research report that looked at the results of the pre-emption of Anti-Predatory Lending laws. The share of high-cost (usurious) loans increased from 16 percent in 2004, to 46 percent in 2007. High-cost loans defaulted in unusually higher numbers. There was a significantly lower rate of defaults for mortgage loans that actually considered a borrower's ability to repay, limited fees and penalties, and had lower interest rates. The report just reinforces good old common sense. When someone enters into a contract trying to screw the other party, things usually end up bad. When both parties to a contract are treated with fairness, honesty, and respect, things usually work out for the best.

When bankers figured out how to rob future cash flow, their usurious profits were stupendous; unmatched in history. That created another problem – how to hide the money. The answer was not difficult: take the MBS, chop it, dice it, slice it, mix it up with other derivatives that included cash flow from credit card debt, auto loans, and student loans, and then repackage the mess as a CLO, CDO, or some other form of derivative. Soon they were creating synthetic derivatives, modelled to replicate a derivative with an actual underlying asset (such as a mortgage). To follow the paper trail would have required the ability to turn apple sauce back into apples.

There was another problem: taxes. Again, the answer was not difficult: move the derivatives off-balance sheet and eventually move them off-shore. By 2007, 83 of the 100 largest corporations in the United States had subsidiaries in off-shore tax havens. All the big banks had multiple subsidiaries in multiple off-shore tax havens such as the Cayman Islands or the Channel Islands.

In 2007, Deutsche Bank attempted to foreclose on 14 homeowners in Ohio. The homeowners fought back. The judge, Christopher Boyko, tried to determine who actually held the mortgage note from each of the individual homeowners. The results were mind boggling. In the case of Carol Moore, a homeowner, court records show her $77,000 mortgage was bundled, sliced, diced and sold 660 times in less than one year. The entities that purchased all or part of that mortgage included: #157 BT MH Finance in the Cayman Islands, #176 Great Future International Limited in the British Virgin Islands, #177 Bocaina LP in the Cayman Islands, #179 Arvoredo Investments in the Cayman Islands, #180 BTVR Investments No.1 Limited in the Channel Islands, #213 Liberty Investments Limited in the Cayman Islands, and the list goes on for more than 20 pages.

Who owns these partnerships? It has been widely speculated that upper level executives of Deutsche, Goldman Sachs, Morgan Stanley, Bear Stearns, AIG, (etc.,) owned these partnerships; also, some politicians held partnerships in their "blind trusts". Rather than identify the true parties behind the façade of Cayman Island Partnerships, Deutsche Bank gave Carol Moore her house free and clear. The plaintiffs chose to walk away rather than have their scheme exposed for what it really is – fraud and tax evasion!

And where were the regulators during all this? The Federal Reserve is one of the main regulators of banks. Fed Chairman Greenspan was philosophically opposed to regulation; which is kind of like having a Pope that's opposed to religion. Christopher Cox, the former Chairman of the SEC believed his role was to oversee the "voluntary regulation" of Wall Street and the ratings agencies. Taking a page from Nero's playbook he claimed his "greatest contribution" during the inevitable crisis was staying "calm." The Bush administration was busy looking for WMDs in Iraq and they hardly bothered to look for CDOs in the Cayman Islands; besides, they were "business friendly".

The banking lobby had been hammering away at regulations for years; they had personally written legislation (from South Dakota's laws to strike down usury, to the Financial Modernization Act); the bankers had spent billions in campaign contributions; and they had established a revolving door from government to cushy corporate jobs. Problems solved. What could go wrong?

Chapter 10

The Meltdown – The Ponzi Scheme Unravels

The inevitable undoing of any Ponzi Scheme, or pyramid, is
that eventually you run out of suckers; and then the whole mess
collapses. Over-borrowing and over-lending always end badly.
Eventually people stopped paying exorbitant prices for houses and
subprime borrowers stopped paying on predatory loans. Default and
delinquency rates began to rise in 2006, but the pace of lending did not
slow. Leverage is a money-making scheme when prices go up, the
profits are multiplied by the amount of leverage; when prices go
down, the losses are multiplied by the amount of leverage. Bear
Stearns was one of the early players to experience the multiplier effect
of deleveraging. Bear ran several hedge funds, including the Bear
Stearns High Grade Structured Credit Strategies Fund, and its riskier
sister offering, the High Grade Structured Credit Strategies Enhanced
Leverage Fund. What could go wrong? They were high grade; they
were structured; they had strategies; they had leverage; they were
enhanced; enhanced is good. They went broke in June 2007.

At first the Federal Reserve and the Treasury told us the
Subprime Mortgage Implosion would be a minor blip, no more than a
$40 billion dollar problem:

March 13th, 2007 - "the fallout in subprime mortgages is going to be painful to some lenders, but it is largely contained." – Treasury Secretary Henry Paulson.

March 28th, 2007 - "At this juncture . . . the impact on the broader economy and financial markets of the problems in the subprime markets seems likely to be contained," - Federal Reserve Chairman Ben Bernanke.

April 20th, 2007 - "I don't see (subprime mortgage market troubles) imposing a serious problem. I think it's going to be largely contained." And, "All the signs I look at" show "the housing market is at or near the bottom," -- Henry Paulson.

June 20th, 2007 - (the subprime fallout) ``will not affect the economy overall." – Ben Bernanke.

The economic forecasting skills of the Federal Reserve, Treasury, and most economists proved to be as useful as a bicycle for a fish. This leaves three possible conclusions about the government's complicity in the credit collapse: 1) they were incredibly incompetent, 2) they allowed it to happen, 3) they were involved in making it happen.

The banks realized they were highly leveraged and they were bleeding red ink. They knew that other banks were no better off, and therefore no bank could be considered a safe trading partner. To staunch the losses, banks stopped buying toxic asset from one another.

Credit markets started to freeze. Money market funds posted losses; long considered a safe place to park money, they "broke the buck," dropping below the baseline of $1 per share. Financial institutions lost confidence in one another. Money stopped circulating.

The foreclosures continued and not just in the United States; a British bank, Northern Rock collapsed; customers lined up on the sidewalk in a classic run on the bank; the bank was nationalized.

Rather than ride to the rescue of Main Street, the Fed decided to help their banking buddies by injecting $200 billion in capital into the credit markets. In March 2008, Bear Stearns collapsed. The Fed staved off a Bear Stearns bankruptcy by assuming $30 billion in liabilities and orchestrating a sale to JPMorgan Chase for pennies on the dollar. The government did not allow Bear Stearns to go into bankruptcy because Bear had written trillions of dollars of Credit Default Swaps, and there were massive bets against Bear Stearns; bankruptcy would be considered default, which would have triggered CDS payouts. The counterparty risk that all Bear's trading partners were exposed to was so far, and wide, and deep, that if Bear were to enter bankruptcy it would've taken years to sort out the risk and losses. That was an untenable option.

Several small banks failed. In the summer of 2008, California based IndyMac (which was original formed by Angelo Mozillo of Countrywide infamy) was taken over by the FDIC; customers lined up on the sidewalk in a classic run on the bank; FDIC insured depositors eventually got their money; uninsured depositors lost about a billion dollars. One depositor was told to transfer $12 million dollars as proof of funds for a down payment for a loan that IndyMac promised to fund; later in the day the bank was seized. The depositor was only insured for $100,000 by the FDIC. He was offered $6 million as a settlement, and has sued the FDIC and IndyMac. No one has lost any money in FDIC insured accounts – yet. But depositors have lost more than $2 billion in bank accounts that exceeded the FDIC insurance limits.

In July 2008, the Bush Administration came to the rescue of Main Street with the Hope for Homeowners Act and promises of $300 billion in loan guarantees; over the following six months this program was able to refinance 25 mortgages nationwide. Another mission accomplished.

By August of 2008, Fannie Mae and Freddie Mac were on the brink of collapse; the Treasury took them over. In September, investment banker Lehman Brothers was following in the path of Bear Stearns, but the Fed did not step in to cut a deal. Lehman had been a fierce competitor with its larger rival Goldman Sachs. Treasury Secretary Henry Paulson was the former CEO of Goldman. Paulson was adamantly opposed to a bailout for Lehman. Merrill Lynch appeared ready to collapse. Paulson and Bernanke forced Bank of America to acquire Merrill.

Lehman collapsed. Lehman was just one investment bank, granted it was big – with $630 billion or so in liabilities, but when it collapsed the entire financial system appeared on the verge of collapse. The Treasury and the Federal Reserve were pumping money towards banks and investment banks in the hopes of restoring confidence, but the banks had lost their most valuable asset – trust.

The largest US insurance company, American International Group, AIG, was getting hammered. AIG was much bigger than Lehman and did more business on a global basis. AIG had written more than $440 billion worth of bad swaps on corporate bonds and mortgage-backed securities. As the value of these insured-referenced entities fell, AIG had massive write-downs and had to post more collateral. AIG's ratings were downgraded and the company had to post even more collateral, which it didn't have. One small AIG corporate subsidiary blew apart the largest insurance company in the world. The government pumped $85 billion into AIG to keep it floating.

Derivatives continued to default. Goldman Sachs played both sides of the trade, selling mortgages as a safe investment, and also buying CDS "insurance", betting the mortgage portfolios would fail. They were shorting what they had just sold. Anybody who has ever tried to collect on an insurance claim knows that insurance companies regularly challenge those claims. When Goldman Sachs put in its claim for collection on CDS insurance there were no questions and no challenges. AIG, in a very un-insurance company manner, paid off the

CDS "insurance" claim to the investment bankers. Four months later Goldman Sachs collected $12.9 billion on CDS claims.

Taxpayers now owned Fannie Mae, Freddie Mac, and a large chunk of AIG. Bear Stearns, Lehman Brothers, and Merrill Lynch had essentially collapsed.

Central bankers around the world decided to coordinate efforts. They pledged $180 billion dollars to shore up money market funds, trying to avert a run. The Federal Reserve also pumped $105 billion into the US banking system. In the 112 days following the collapse of Lehman, the Fed doubled the currency and cash reserves in the nation's banks.

Chapter 11

Treason at the Treasury – The Coup

On Friday, September 19, 2008, Treasury Secretary Henry Paulson put together a 3 page, partially scrawled document laying out a plan to spend $700 billion to buy faulty mortgage related assets and raise the national debt limit – all without judicial oversight. Paulson and Bernanke held conference calls and closed door, deal making sessions with politicians, warning that the global financial system was on the verge of a meltdown. Standing before the television cameras, looking as nervous as a suicide bomber with a vest of dynamite strapped to his chest, Paulson announced his scheme. If the government did not pay hundreds of billions to the banks, the bomb would detonate and destroy 401k, pension plans, jobs, and civilization in general. Paulson looked scared and he sold his package of fear. It was the biggest heist in history; hundreds of billions stolen from taxpayers and stuffed into the pockets of bankers.

The big banks got bigger. JPMorgan Chase took over the largest Savings and Loan, Washington Mutual. Citigroup agreed to buy Wachovia. Wells Fargo would eventually top Citi's offer and acquire all of Wachovia. Goldman Sachs tried to buy Citi.

Paulson's three-page ransom note went to Congress, which rewrote the mess, rejected it, and then eventually passed a new version. On October 3, 2008, President Bush signed the bill into law, only after Republicans won provisions to ease accounting rules for banks. Wall Street continued to wet its pants. In the following week, the Dow Jones Industrial Average lost 1,874 points or 20% of its value.

The financial system did not collapse but it continued to teeter. The banks didn't know what they had on the books, and what they had off the books they couldn't calculate the value, if any. Paulson's plan called for the banks to drive their beat up rusted out clunker to the Fed discount window and they could exchange it for a brand new Cadillac. But the bankers couldn't find the keys or the title to the clunker, or maybe they were afraid there were some skeletons stuffed in the trunk. The credit markets remained frozen.

Ten days after Congress approved the bailout, Paulson changed the terms; instead of buying the banks' toxic assets, he decided it was best to inject $125 billion into the banks to signal the government would not let the banks fail. The nine largest banks were recapitalized on the same day behind closed doors. And that was followed by more bailouts. And when the big banks continued to teeter, they received even more taxpayer dollars. The potential for failure was painted as financial Armageddon. The government declared certain financial institutions "too big to fail." The banks faced with insolvency took the money (of course) and did one of two things: they hoarded the bailout money to the detriment of commerce, or they made risky bets to try and return to solvency. Both tacks merely put salt on a wound.

Meanwhile, on Main Street foreclosures continued and jobs were being lost, but middle class families and small businesses were apparently too small to sweat.

The exact amount spent, or allocated to be spent, to shore up banks is still uncertain; the estimates range from $2.5 trillion spent to $24 trillion committed. Rather than protecting citizens caught up in a predatory loan induced bubble, the government tried to protect the profits of the usurers. The banks have been sucking up the cash like a black hole, while doing nothing to alter their risky business practices. The consequences may only be clear through the lens of history, but it is already clear that there was a massive redistribution of wealth. In populist revolts, wealth is typically redistributed from the wealthy elite to the peasant masses; in this case the profits were privatized and the losses were socialized, and the money went from the masses to the wealthy elite.

There are three types of conquest: war, religious conquest, and economic conquest. In economic conquests the public is forced to pay tribute; it requires no standing army, no guns, no police, no visible force. The captive are required to pay tribute to the captors and the tribute is collected as taxes and legal debt. Those that pay tribute believe they are paying for protection from some, perhaps unseen, enemy. The captors become the benefactors and protectors. When Paulson opened the vaults of the Treasury he committed treason. The bankers were given mountains of money and also the power behind the money; a power rightly reserved to a government of the people.

For years, the banks had built their business on a foundation of usury, instituted fractional reserves and developed other vehicles for leverage, and they had jacked up interest rates by tearing down consumer protections. The mega-banks that funded the subprime industry were not victims of an unforeseen financial collapse. These banks were deliberate enablers that bankrolled the predatory lending that threatened the financial system. Twenty one of the top 25 subprime lenders were financed by banks that received bailout money. The bankers made out like bandits, and so far they have made a clean getaway.

How? One of the effects of usury is to centralize wealth, and as wealth became centralized, a tight bond was made between government and their private sector allies. Slowly and subtly large corporations started running the country like a for-profit company and they are the shareholders. This is common practice for emerging economies, banana republics, and dictatorships; it is now the status quo in the United States.

Chapter 12

Corporatist Politics – One Political Party: A Confederacy of Greedy Dunces

What would be called bribery in a third world dictatorship is called campaign finance and lobbying in the US and it is a big business. Lobbyists set up shop right down the street from Congress and spend billions of dollars annually to manipulate legislation, regulations, and judicial decisions. And when lobbying efforts are not enough, the private sector actually takes over positions of power in government. There is a revolving door between government jobs and private sector jobs. A former federal employee can find lucrative employment as a lobbyist, a consultant, or strategist – provided they were cooperative with the private sector when they were in the government's employ.

The list of public officials with past or future ties to big business reads like a government phone book, almost every name is included: Don Regan (Merrill Lynch), Nicolas Brady (Dillon Read), Robert Rubin (Goldman, Citigroup), Henry Paulson (Goldman), Alan Greenspan (Pimco), Dick Cheney (Halliburton), Phil Gramm (UBS). Senator Chris Dodd accepted preferential mortgages loans from Countrywide, part of the "Friends of Angelo" program that Countrywide offered to politicians, celebrities, and newsmakers. The guy from Citigroup can talk to the guy from Goldman and the guy from Hartford Insurance and the other guy from Merrill – and they never have to step out of the Treasury building. And while it might not make sense to appoint Joe the plumber as Treasury Secretary, it doesn't make sense to expect altruistic public service from people who face the temptations of big payoffs. It is equally ludicrous to think politicians are ignorant of the holdings in their "blind trusts". They might be doing the peoples' business or they might be doing their own business. Even the most high minded allow unique access to business buddies. The truth is that Fed Chairman Bernanke and Treasury Secretary Geithner speak to Wall Street bankers on a daily basis. When a problem occurs they talk to the bankers. When the bankers want something, they talk to the Secretary and the Chairman. Normal citizens do not have this kind of access. Elected Senators and Representatives do not have this kind of access.

The result is Corporatist capitalism. And in this case, the elite financial interests that created the crisis now control how the mess will be addressed, either because they are now in government positions of power or because they have purchased influence. While tighter regulation, greater transparency, stricter accounting, and indictments might seem like reasonable responses for the near destruction of the economy, that has not been the case; instead the response has been to shower the perpetrators with cash, big bonuses, little or no increase in regulation, looser accounting standards, lucrative trading opportunities, and greater political influence. Politicians know that if they stand up to the banking and corporate special interests, then the traders on Wall Street can punish them in one day by driving prices down, and issuing a press release that says the politicians have hurt peoples' 401K and IRA. The citizens get scared and Wall Street wins.

Once the financial elites influence had smothered government, it spread to media and the culture as a whole. The mantra was "greed is good" and "what's good for Wall Street is good for America"; both lines are lies. What's good for Wall Street is only good for Wall Street. The stock market is not the economy, even though bloated bankers see themselves at the center of, and masters of the universe. The red and green digital tickers do not reflect the real economy but a grotesque distortion. When the wealth of America is centralized in the pockets of the financial elite on Wall Street, that's where the money stays; it does not trickle back to Portland or Pascagoula. The notion that greed is good is just obscene and has been unacceptable for thousands of years.

A government falling under the control of financial elites is not a wild conspiracy theory; it is nothing new. It happened in ancient

Venice and 17th century England; it was a major factor in the
American Revolution; it is commonplace in third world countries; and
it has been a constant challenge for the United States. President
Andrew Jackson was correct when he cast shame on the bankers for
what they had done, but he had the courage to stand up to them so that
no shame would be cast on him for the further damage they would
have wrecked. He certainly did not give them bonuses.

"Less than 24 hours after his swearing-in ceremony, U.S.
Treasury Secretary Timothy F. Geithner surprised Camden R. Fine
with an invitation to a one-on-one meeting about the financial crisis. "I
about fell out of my chair," said Fine, president of the Independent
Community Bankers of America, a Washington-based trade group
with about 5,000 members. He was in a corner office overlooking the
White House at the Treasury Department the next morning, telling
Geithner that behemoths such as Citigroup Inc. and Bank of America
Corp. were a menace, he said. "They should be broken up and sold
off," Fine, 58, said he declared, as Geithner scribbled notes before
thanking him for his time and ushering him out into the January chill.
The Treasury secretary didn't follow through on Fine's suggestion, just
as he didn't act on the advice of former Federal Reserve Chairman
Paul A. Volcker, or Federal Deposit Insurance Corp. head Sheila C.
Bair, or the dozens of economists and politicians who pressed the
White House for measures that would limit the size or activities of
U.S. banks. One year after the demise of Lehman Brothers Holdings
Inc. paralyzed the financial system, "mega-banks," as Fine's group
calls them, are as interconnected and inscrutable as ever. The Obama

administration's plan for a regulatory overhaul wouldn't force them to shrink or simplify their structure." - Bloomberg

We have a new phenomenon – mega-banks that are "Too big to fail". The concern is moral hazard. The idea is simple. If you are continually willing to protect people from the consequences of their own errors, your benevolence will be factored into the future decisions of the persons rescued. The protected party becomes averse to risk and they engage in riskier and riskier behavior. In the long run, they will make even more errors. The principle exists at all levels. The teacher who changes grades when students plead hardship isn't helping in the long run. The teacher is rewarding and thereby encouraging poor study habits. He is creating moral hazard. The central banker who bails out banks whose incompetence has resulted in massive losses isn't helping in the long run. The central banker is rewarding the banks for gambling, thereby creating a moral hazard.

For centuries some banks have made big profits and some banks have failed. When a bank fails, it goes out of business and some clever scoundrel eventually comes along and opens a new bank. But in the recent drama, the government decided that certain banks were simply too big to fail; if they were to fail, they would drag everyone's deposits and pension plans and the entire financial system into an abyss. The bankers had become domestic enemies, more dangerous than terrorists. This should have been clear evidence that the banks had misused depositors' money. Indictments should have been forthcoming. Instead, the government surrendered to the banks' demands.

The great Republic that had withstood the loss of Presidents to assassins' bullets, which had held strong even with the loss of millions of brave heroes on battlefields, suddenly found that the one indispensible element to the survival of the nation was the banks. The coup was accomplished. The government was no longer of the people, by the people, for the people; now it was government of the bankers, by the bankers, for the bankers. The bankers had gambled and failed, and they looted the Treasury, and continued gambling. For years the bankers had peddled influence, written legislation, were allowed to mint money (or at least create it out of thin air with fractional reserve banking), and generally exempt themselves from regulation. As the politicians opened the Treasury vaults to be looted by the bankers it became clear, or at least there was a vague uneasiness, that our democratic republic had been taken over.

The Republicans blamed the Democrats; the Democrats blamed the Republicans; and behind the smoke and mirrors of name calling and incivility we lost sight that the bickering only served to divide the country and hide the fact that the guilty party was the usurers. The nastiness covered the fact that our democratic republic was no longer represented by a two party system; we had morphed into a three party system: on the far right was a handful of Conservatives, on the far left was a handful of Progressives, and the big majority is full of Corporatists – politicians that had sold out to corporations, politicians that hoped to sell out to corporations, politicians that had swallowed the Blue Pill and accepted the propaganda that corporations were benign benefactors and not cruel oligarchs.

The Democratic Party and the Republican Party have morphed into one party – the Corporatists. They are a confederacy of dunces controlled by money that pours in from corporations. Money is necessary to be re-elected and the politicians don't dare do anything that would upset the corporations and result in the money spigot being turned off. The Democratic Corporatists are flooded with money from the same sources that flood the Republican Corporatists. The money isn't given to the politicians to support a Democratic/Progressive agenda or a Republican/Conservative agenda; the money is given to support a Corporatist agenda; the agenda is simple – more money for the Corporatists; pump up the quarterly balance sheets, collect the bonus and get out of Dodge before the dust settles. The vast majority of politicians are Corporatists and they serve the narrow interests of a narrow set of economic interests. These narrow interests influence the outcomes of elections; they write legislation; they make sure neither side gets too uppity.

Chapter 13

Corporate Personhood – Do Corporations Dream?

The source of corporate involvement in politics goes back to laws that give personhood to corporations. Even though corporations are abstractions, have special protections from liabilities, and are not limited to a natural lifespan, they have created a super-person with the potential for something like immortality. This is a strange power for an entity that is never mentioned in the Constitution. By achieving this designation of corporations as persons, real flesh and blood people are relegated to subhuman status. The Constitution only mentions We the People and the government; it says nothing about We the Corporations or We the Investment Bankers. Corporations are legal entities; machines for getting a job done; they have no soul; they can't dream. Corporate Personhood is the legal fiction that property is a person. This is just as absurd as the legal fiction of slavery, which determines that people are property. For many years in this country it was not just slaves that were considered property, but also Native Americans, immigrants, poor people, and women.

Santa Clara County v. Southern Pacific Railroad 1886 arguably decided 14th Amendment rights providing equal protection under the law applied to corporations. *Minneapolis & St Louis Railroad v. Beckwith* 1889 ruled that corporations are persons for both process and equal protection. *Noble v. Union River Logging,* 1893, gave corporations 5th Amendment rights to due process of law. These cases gave corporations personhood before personhood was granted to women and people of color. In 1906, corporations got 4th Amendment search and seizure protection (*Hale v. Henkel*). In 1922, they got the "takings" clause of the 5th Amendment (*Pennsylvania Coal Co. v. Mahon*), and a regulatory law was deemed to be "takings." In 1947, they started getting First Amendment protections (Taft-Hartley Act). In 1976, the Supreme Court determined that money spent for political purposes is equal to exercising free speech, and since "corporate persons" have First Amendment rights, they can basically contribute as much money as they want to political parties and candidates (*Buckley v. Valeo*).

Individual citizens have no hope of matching the money of corporations. Corporations have special advantages when earning money, plus tax advantages, plus liability to prevent losses. If money is considered free speech, there is no way individual citizens' voice can be as loud and powerful as corporations. In politics, money doesn't talk, it screams, it drowns the voices of merely mortal citizens. The concept that corporations are persons also means that corporations can govern – not with a vote, but with political manipulation.

Dick Durbin, the number two Democrat in the Senate, admitted: "And the banks - hard to believe in a time when we're facing a banking crisis that many of the banks created - are still the most powerful lobby on Capitol Hill. And they frankly own the place."

"Corporatists" refers to big corporations, capable of throwing their weight around, not to small businesses that have incorporated. Merely being employed by a large corporation does not make you a Corporatist, but it might make you vulnerable.

Slavery, skin color, and gender once kept wages nonexistent or at poverty levels. Now, bank bailouts steal money away from the majority and funnel it into the pockets of an elite few. Just as sharecropping and the company store once kept people trapped in permanently subservient production roles; now, predatory mortgage loans, credit card debt, consumer debt, and payday loans keep millions on Americans in permanent debt, to feed interest payments to the world's richest, while their own families live in poverty and lose their homes to foreclosure. The laws that protect real people from abuses by corporations are now written by corporations.

Corporate ownership of the political process is not limited to banks. GE is the largest single corporate lobbyist. General Electric Vice Chairman John G. Rice distributed a memo in August 2009, calling for GE workers to join the General Electric Political Action Committee: "GEPAC is an important tool that enables GE employees to collectively help support candidates who share the values and goals of GE." The letter explains how GE "worked closely" with authors of specific legislation. This means GE wrote the legislation. The full letter suggests that "share the values and goals of GE" really means "support policies that profit the company." Should a GE employee support policy that profits GE, even if she believes that policy is harmful to her family or her nation or her personal morals? Well, if she wants to keep her job, the answer is clear.

To call the Corporatists whores is an insult to whores. The Corporatist politicians not only sell their principles and their integrity to the highest bidder, they also sell their sacred vote. What makes this more despicable is that politicians have the power to send our sons and daughters, husbands and wives, brothers and neighbors into battle to protect and defend…what? Corporate interests or freedom? There is no place for bribery in politics, even if it is hidden under the name of campaign contributions and lobbying.

The Corporatists are easy to identify; they are politicians that accept corporate donations, jobs for themselves, and jobs for their staff; they are the corporate honchos and lobbyists that pass out the bribes. It is really that simple. The politicians do what is demanded by those that supply the resources. Politicians can only serve one master. They can claim they are not influenced by corporate largesse but this is a lie, even if they believe the lie.

Chapter 14

Plutonomists – The Super Rich Have a Solution: "Let Them Eat Cake"

It is not just the Corporatists. Citigroup was kind enough to supply a name for the super-rich who try to manipulate the economy: Plutonomists. They defined plutonomy as an economy that is run by and for the ultra-wealthy; nobody else matters. There is no "average" consumer in Plutonomies. There is only the rich "and everyone else."

There are rich consumers, few in number, but disproportionate in the gigantic slice of income and consumption they take. There are the rest, the "non-rich", the multitudinous many, but only accounting for surprisingly small bites of the national pie. The Citigroup report clearly endorses inequality, and determines that Plutonomists should be targeted as Citi customers.

The research report stated: "The top 1% of households in the U.S., (about 1 million households) accounted for about 20% of overall U.S. income in 2000, slightly smaller than the share of income of the bottom 60% of households put together. That's about 1 million households compared with 60 million households, both with similar slices of the income pie. The top 1% of households also account for 33% of net worth, greater than the bottom 90% of households put together. It gets better (or worse, depending on your political stripe) -

the top 1% of households account for 40% of *financial* net worth, more than the bottom 95% of households put together. The Managerial Aristocracy, like in the Gilded Age, the Roaring Twenties, and the thriving nineties, needs to commandeer a vast chunk of that rising profit share, either through capital income, or simply paying itself a lot."

"At the heart of plutonomy, is income inequality. Societies that are willing to tolerate/endorse income inequality are willing to tolerate/endorse plutonomy." The Citigroup report warns their wealthy clients that there is a risk that inequality will not be tolerated, but they go on to say they are not concerned – the propaganda machine is still spinning. "Perhaps one reason that societies allow plutonomy is because enough of the electorate believe they have a chance of becoming a Plutoparticipant. Why kill it off, if you can join it? In a sense this is the embodiment of the "American dream"."

The reality is that every child that ever played organized sports has a greater chance of becoming a major league star than becoming a Plutoparticipant; a greater chance of being struck by lightning; and your odds are better at hitting the Lotto.

One way to eliminate plutonomy is through progressive taxation, an idea thoroughly renounced by Citigroup. And the biggest fear for the Plutonomists is democracy, because the poor, huddled masses outnumber the super-rich in the voting booths. The report says the ultra-wealthy should not concern themselves; as long as the

Plutonomists give the *appearance* of honesty, "there is little threat". And of course, the uber-rich can always buy influence in elections. Spending millions to advertise your candidate is equivalent to having millions of votes, but the reality is that it is buying the election.

Bank of America issued a similar report that concluded the well-heeled might be able to save the US economy from a long period of dismally weak consumer spending—if only we don't jack up their taxes. The consumer debt problem is a problem only for the middle class, or what's left of it. The super-wealthy don't have a debt problem. (The super-wealthy are the usurers.)

The Bank of America report was entitled: "The Myth of the Overlevered Consumer." The Citigroup report is entitled: "Plutonomy: Buying Luxury, Explaining Global Imbalances." Apparently they decided against: "Let Them Eat Cake."

Chapter 15

Greed – You Can't Serve Two Masters

"No servant can serve two masters. He will either hate one and love the other, or be devoted to one and despise the other. You cannot serve God and mammon" – Matt. 6:24. Most people do not know what mammon means. In the broad sense, mammon means greed, the culture of greed, or the love of money. In a more specific interpretation, the poet John Milton presents Mammon as one of the devils cast out of heaven, a lesser brother of Satan:

"Mammon, the least erected spirit that fell

From heaven; for even in Heaven his looks and thoughts

Were always downward bent, admiring more

The riches of heaven's pavement, trodden gold,

Than aught divine or holy else enjoyed

In vision beatific."

- Paradise Lost, Book I

Mammon subordinates character and virtue and liberty and human life to sordid gain, yet he holds the sceptre of power. People are valued for the money they command, not for their deeds or character. Meanwhile the victims of our dishonest money system proliferate while we are told that justice and equity has no place in commercial life. The debt collector, the repo man, the politician that sells his vote, and the banker foreclosing on a home may feel some remorse, but it is cast aside because "it's not personal, it's business"; this is a line from the movie *The Godfather*; this is the justification of gangsters and CEOs. This is a very modern approach that the greatest minds of not just this age but any age would find repugnant.

The bankers, in their role as predatory usurers and usurpers of public trust, bear the vast majority of blame for the current economic crisis and the longer term decline of the economy, but the borrower must bear some responsibility, even though it is difficult to escape the temptations of Mammon. The American consumer bought the sales pitch much like Adam and Eve succumbed to the temptation of forbidden fruit; just as some Americans once bought the idea that slavery was good. The person who is offered a loan is usually greatly delighted. The loan seems to be the vehicle to escape emergencies or an opportunity to secure greater results. There is hope that the newfound resources will tear down the walls that have limited and restrained. The usurers dangle opportunity like a serpent dangles the apple. There is a sense of freedom and exhilaration in tearing down the prison walls, but the delight is transient because the debt binds like a ball and chain; the borrower becomes the servant of the lender and usury makes the servant a slave.

It is not just the usurers and the borrowers that share the blame. The politicians have made an unholy alliance to further their political ambitions by receiving billions of dollars in political contributions, then selling out the American citizens who elected them; all for the benefit of the corporate elite. The radical thinking of the Founding Fathers was that People are important, not the aristocrats, nobility, corporations, and financial elite that usurped the will of the People. America, in only 250 years, has systematically stripped the power of the People for the benefit of the few, the wealthy, the new corporate aristocrats and bankers.

We have slipped into a state of seemingly inescapable usury. The arguments and wisdom of abolishing usury may seem quaint and antiquated; maybe the prohibitions were righteous and beneficent in their time but now they seem an unjust, inapplicable, even discriminatory impediment to commerce and advancement. There have been magnificent innovations in transportation, medicine, communication, and technology as commerce has spread globally. Finance, even usurious finance, is considered the lubricant for the engine of commerce. To revive prohibitions on usury would have the effect of turning civilization backward; as crazy as asking someone to abandon cars, telephones, and electricity. Usury did not create technological advances, people did.

The advancements of the recent past are far from universal. Half the world's population lives in extreme poverty. For the past century, the world has not been free of war somewhere in the world, and the planet itself struggles with degradation of the environment. The American middle class, that was the envy of the world after WW II, has been robbed of their hard earned wages and even their jobs, but are left with debt the same as the farmer in ancient times that borrowed money for seed. Americans have seen their standard of living slowly declining. Most are just a paycheck or two from poverty.

Ultimately the changes are minor when compared to the things that are permanent. Human nature has not changed. The things that promote health and happiness are the same now as in ancient times. Discipline, culture, physical and mental exercise, and education add more to human development than a credit card. Your family is still the most important social unit just as it has been for the ages. Your neighborhood and your community are still where you spend most of your time and you gain no great advantage by having your shoes made in a sweatshop half the world away, yet you will find great good in knowing your neighbors and caring for your common interests. Morality has not been repealed. The teachings of Buddha, Krishna, Moses, Jesus, and Mohammed are still valid. Even atheists with no written scripture can see the necessity of strong moral fiber, fairness, and justice. Conscience and compassion can never be silenced by immorality and cruelty. There is still a relation between cause and effect. Plants still need soil and water and sunlight to grow. We have improved our tools but the natural world is essentially the same as it was 4,000 years ago. The nature of money has not changed. Money is still a store of value, a measure of value, and a medium of exchange. Paper money and plastic cards may be more convenient than silver coins or tally sticks but the function is the same. The law of supply and demand has not changed over the years. Honesty and integrity are still essential elements of successful commerce. Money could always be used to purchase the tools to make money in business, but money could never produce anything by itself; food, clothing, shelter, cars, computers, and a thousand other worthwhile objects were always made by the labor of people, not by the sweat and intelligence of a coin or a piece of paper.

The prohibition of usury may seem like a dusty relic. Credit and debt are ubiquitous. Families do not own their homes, businesses do not own their offices or manufacturing plants, farmers do not own their fields. The United States has become the biggest debtor nation in history. That doesn't make usury right. It only shows how much business, commerce, culture, and politics have been enslaved by this practice. If violating a law annuls it, then we can push aside any law; murder, theft, and torture aren't so bad if everybody is doing it. But of course we do have laws, handed down over the ages, and respect for those laws is more than the lubricant for the engine of commerce, it is the very foundation of commerce and civilization.

The very fact that the introduction of rules prohibiting usury comes to us from the Scriptures, purportedly delivered by God to the prophets, makes such concepts suspect in this modern and enlightened age. Many reject the very idea that even if there is a God, His interest or ability to resolve mankind's economic problems is no more than a delusional fantasy. For most of mankind the very idea that God might have provided a solution to economic instability thousands of years ago is only another of the archaic fairy tales that keeps mankind from accepting the inevitably of a boom and bust world; a world of depression and inflation that are the unavoidable earmarks of a capitalistic modern society.

The notion that God's *Anti-usury Program* might well provide a solution to such economic woes appears to be even more ridiculous when even our greatest economists won't bother to give it a serious thought. Yet despite the heavy opposition the imposition of such economic laws inspired over the centuries, the most surprising result was that they really worked and brought about true economic growth and wealth. Strange, too, that not only the Judeo-Christian religions, but virtually every religion has in the past implemented Anti-usury programs for economic and moral stability should give pause to the naysayers.

Some four thousand ago, even as now, the naysayers rally around the theory that neither our personal economy, nor that of the entire world, can function without a financial system based on the payment of interest. The very wheels of progress would surely grind to a halt as industry and development collapse. The fact is that such collapse did not occur; Solomon's kingdom developed a most vibrant economy and brought about unimagined individual wealth; while a wide variety of economic experiments have come and gone, leaving destruction in their wake.

Could it possibly be that in the past a "Wiser Head" actually handed down to mankind a program for economic well being for individuals as well as for nations? Could it possibly be that by the reapplication of usury laws we could actually implement a Golden Age of individual wealth and stability? Could it actually be possible that the elimination of usury might also become a cure for greed and for economic slavery? Would that elimination stimulate a stronger moral backbone to end other causes of human woe? Would the elimination of the excessive interest costs of usury put an end to world hunger?

Actually, the laws against usury had a good track record throughout history. Like government, crime, and gambling, usury has no economic benefit. Rather, by adding another cost, it creates a drag on the economy and development; an un-needed burden. To start to unleash the power of an economy freed from usury we could start with a return to ban *excessive* interest; before moving slowly to a total ban on interest of any amount. Lending freed from interest would evolve into more considered and wiser investments as the lender evolves into an investor.

How could we ascertain of the benefits if we are unwilling to unleash the power of such a system? The naysayers will tell us that it would destroy the world's economy and bring about world hunger and want. The ancient truths revealed that credit with interest served only to increase the cost of goods and services and polarize the population. Eliminating the restraints of the usury laws encourages the worst of man's illiberality and does nothing more than accomplishes a redistribution of wealth from the producer, the worker, to the money lenders who create nothing. Usury is so bound up with injustice that its practice cannot fail to increase the hard conditions of everyone.

**Section Three – Usurious Carnage and Ubiquitous Dirty Tricks
and Their Effect on You, the Consumer**

Chapter 16

Consumer Debt – The Ball and Chain That Strangles

It's everywhere you want to be.

Long live dreams.

Love every day.

All it takes.

The key.

Wherever it takes you, the future takes Visa.

It pays to Discover.

There are some things money can't buy. For everything else there's MasterCard.

Make life rewarding.

My life. My card.

All you need.

What's in your wallet?

Don't leave home without it.

We've all been exposed to the ad copy and it is remarkably good advertising. It tempts you. It inspires you to live, love, discover, and be rewarded. It's a lie, but reality is a tougher sell:

My life. My card. My never-ending debt.

All you don't really need.

The key…, to bankruptcy.

Don't lose your job without it.

You will pay to Discover.

What's in your wallet? Hand it over.

Medical bills: $23,476.52, Auto repair: $547.88, Living debt free: Priceless.

What the large print offers, the fine print takes away.

Americans have a long history of tension between material pleasure and the quest for simplicity. Consumerism won. Consumer spending accounts for 70% of the Gross Domestic Product, or approximately $10 trillion. Consumer debt, non-mortgage debt tied to consumption not production, hovers around $2.5 trillion. Consumer debt is typically unsecured and frequently short term or revolving; as such, it is more expensive. Despite the rare story of someone who uses their credit cards for start-up capital to form a business, the vast majority of consumer debt is borrowing from the future to pay for consumption today.

Best estimates put the cost of excessive usury (above 10%) on consumer debt at $125 billion per year; this does not include mortgages, business loans, national debt, and other forms of debt, plus externalities associated with usury. Revolving credit (which is almost entirely credit cards) stands at $950 billion and payment on that debt chews up 13.9% of disposable income. The cost to service consumer debt (not including mortgages) tops 20% for most households, and for many families the cost of servicing debt far exceeds tax liabilities.

You can argue all day about excessive taxation, but that doesn't hold a candle to usury.

One of the most troubling parts of all that consumer debt is that the consumer never really knows the true price of anything. It has become common for companies to hide the true cost of the product or service they are selling. A cable TV service might start with a promotional price of $29.95, but that doesn't include fees and taxes, and after three months the promotion ends and the price jumps. An airline ticket price doesn't mention airport usage fees, taxes, service fees, and fees for luggage; the price for any given seat on a plane can vary by hundreds of dollars.

Good luck understanding the true cost of having a bank account: maintenance fees, overdraft protection fees, non-sufficient fund fees, teller fees, ATM fees, and much more. And if you purchase on credit the confusion really kicks in. Few people know the interest rate on their credit card, fewer still calculate the time to pay the debt and the interest that will build up, fewer still consider fees and penalties that might build up, and almost no one calculates the effects of inflation on the value of their purchase paid over time. You may consider that the retailer is making a profit but you probably don't consider that merchants are paying the credit card companies.

As a result it is almost impossible to make an accurate comparison and evaluation of competing products. One of the basic concepts of capitalism is that it achieves the most efficient allocation of resources. If a company can produce a quality product at a good price they are more likely to enjoy robust sales and the consumer gets value. Capitalism is supposed to reward efficiency and quality and pricing in an open and competitive market; money flows to good companies and money flows away from bad companies, but it isn't working. Now the rewards go to the best cheaters. You can't get an accurate price, and you don't really know who you are paying and what. Capitalism fails when everything is priceless.

Chapter 17

Credit Cards – A License to Steal

Owning a credit card company is a license to steal. Holding a credit card is giving permission to be robbed. Americans now hold more than 1.5 billion cards that scream out: "rip me off." The stack of credit cards could stretch into space for 70 miles. Three quarters of all households have credit cards but only 30% pay off those cards each month; the debt just rolls over for everybody else.

In the credit card industry a "deadbeat" is a customer who pays off their entire balance every month, never makes a late payment, and never misses a payment. While this may seem like a prudent, conscientious, highly valued customer, that is not the case because the credit card companies do not make as much money off of deadbeats. Credit card companies have even started charging an annual fee for paying on time and not carrying any balance. It's not easy to be a deadbeat. First, the credit card contract is pretty much indecipherable.

The average credit card contract is 31 pages long and is not intended to be read or understood. President Obama, a former Professor of Constitutional Law, calls them "ridiculously confusing contracts". Even if you read the contract, your interpretation may be different from the banks', and if you end up in a dispute, you will probably lose because the banks have privatized a sizeable swath of the legal system. They have taken away your right to have your dispute determined by a judge and jury.

Most of the nation's credit-card companies have clauses in their contracts that require consumers to resolve disputes through arbitration, a private judicial process that is supposed to be fair, cheap, and more efficient than the courts. And who do the private arbiters work for? Recent allegations show cross ownership links between private arbitration firms and debt collection agencies and banks. Arbitrators that rule in favor of the consumer don't stay arbitrators for long. One class action lawsuit filed against a credit card company revealed that the lender won more than 99 percent of the cases that went to arbitration. And even if you do win your privately arbitrated dispute, the results will not be made public. No one can use your case to establish a precedent for their case. The banks can repeat the same bad behavior time after time after time with no constraints. Consumers have to reinvent the wheel with every case. These kangaroo courts threaten to undermine the legal system and take away one of your most basic rights – justice.

The deck is clearly stacked in favor of the credit card companies. So why tempt fate and apply for a credit card? Several reasons; without a credit card you will pay more for many basic services such as electricity, water, insurance (auto, health, property, casualty, and life), and car rentals. Credit cards are also part of establishing credit scores which determine what you pay for a mortgage, other credit, and even impact your ability to get a job. If you are thrifty and frugal and have a perfect payment history, using only cash or checks, you are considered a credit risk – not suitable for a fair rate on a mortgage, and not suitable for many jobs.

The credit card companies tempt you, not just with the catchy advertising slogans but with direct mail, eight billion preapproved credit card applications each year. Approximately 90 million households have credit cards and those households have more than $10,000 average credit card debt. It may be tempting to think you can get a 30 day loan and pay nothing for it, but it is not easy being a deadbeat.

If a card holder happens to be late on just one payment, things turn really nasty; interest rates are increased, minimum monthly payments can be increased, the borrower's credit rating will drop, and of course fees will be added. The borrower is truly trapped. And that's just what the banks want because that is where they make their biggest profits.

The abuses of the credit card companies have been so bad that in 2009, reforms were enacted to rein in some of the most egregious problems. Credit card companies can no longer hike interest rates if you are late on a non-credit card payment elsewhere; in the past they could hike your credit card interest rate if you were late paying your utility bill (this was called universal default); they can still hike interest rates (for no reason at all) but now they have to tell you in advance (45 day notice is required); they can't hike rates retroactively unless you are 60 days late; they must credit your payment on the day they receive the payment (not hold it for a day and kick it into a late pay); they must send you a bill in a timely manner (no more opening the mail to find that the payment was due yesterday). The bankers' response was to raise interest rates across the board, increase minimum monthly payments, impose annual fees, and to take away available credit even for the most responsible borrowers. For many people, the arbitrary cut in credit limits resulted in; you guessed it, over-limit fees. The reforms are probably a step in the right direction but they failed to address the most basic problem – usury. Usury refers to any gain on a loan, including interest and fees. It is not uncommon for interest rates to top 35% and for fees to be added on, and the addition of fees can push the real rate paid to astronomical levels.

Chapter 18

Fees, Fees, and UnFair Isaac – Sneaky Fees and Dirty Little Credit Secrets

Overdraft fees at US banks and credit unions grew an estimated 70% from 2004 to 2006 — from $10.3 billion to $17.5

billion, according to a study by the Center for Responsible Lending. In 2006, consumers paid $17.5 billion in overdraft fees on just $15.8 billion worth of overdrafts. In 2009, the fees topped $38 billion; enough to send $1526 to every man, woman, and child in Texas. Americans pay more in overdraft fees than the actual amounts by which they overdraw their accounts – the penalty is truly worse than the crime.

Americans make $1.8 trillion in credit card purchases each year and merchants pay the credit card companies more than $45 billion, or more than $400 a year per American household, or about 2.5% of all credit card related sales (the third highest expense for retailers). This is called an interchange fee; this is a fee that is typically charged to everyone, even if they pay cash. When you buy gasoline, more profit goes to the credit card company than to your neighborhood gas station owner. For unexplained reasons, Visa and MasterCard charge 0.3% interchange fees outside the US. Let's be clear. The interchange fee represents a $40 billion dollar tax on the American consumer.

A debit card doesn't carry interest rates because you are only accessing money from your own account, but if you inadvertently make a loan, drawing out more than is in the account, the charges quickly become excessive. If you have $100 in an account and you deposit a $100 check late on a Friday afternoon ($200 total deposited) and over the rest of the weekend you make ten $10 withdrawals plus one $95 withdrawal, you have withdrawn $195. You might think this is not a problem; hold on. Deposits may take three business days or more to clear and be credited to your account; withdrawals are debited the same day and typically from largest to smallest, meaning the first debit is $95, the second debit is $10 and that overdraws the account and results in an overdraft fee; and the remaining nine withdrawals each result in overdraft fees. The typical overdraft fee is $35 and the total fees in this example are $350. You might argue that you had deposited the money and should not be charged any penalty, but you would lose that arbitrated argument 99% of the time because it is explained in the fine print of the contract you never read. The banks are under no obligation to let you know that you have reached the limit of your account. The transaction is approved. You get hit for fees. Due to an accounting glitch you took out a short-term, 3-day loan for $95 and were charged $350 or 271% which works out to an annualized rate of 32,972%. The difference between loan sharks and banks is that banks are licensed to steal.

There are more problems with debit cards. Credit card holders aren't on the hook for fraudulent use of their cards and can challenge charges on goods and services not delivered as promised. Debit card holders aren't guaranteed those same protections. Credit card borrowers face a maximum liability of $50 regardless of when they discover potential fraud. Debit card holders' liability is limited to $50 only if they report perceived fraud within two days; the liability jumps to a maximum $500 from that point to 60 days, and is unlimited thereafter.

Consumers are more worried about banks raiding their accounts than criminals. Consumers are five times more likely to switch banks because of hidden fees than security concerns, according to the survey conducted by the Gartner consulting firm. One in six US adult consumers — an estimated 28 million people — said unexpected fees make them more upset or aggravated than identity theft.

You could always cut up your credit cards and close your account but that will cost you. Your credit score will drop. How much? Nobody knows. It's a secret. How is your credit rating calculated? That's also a secret. Fair Isaac and Beacon are responsible for generating credit scores, also known as FICO scores (for Fair Isaac Co., which should really be called UnFair Isaac); and the methodology is considered proprietary. We do know the general guidelines. Late payments lower the score. Bankruptcy lowers the score (so much for a fresh start). Too much available credit can lower the score. Too little available credit can lower the score. And plain, old fashioned, ugly discrimination can lower the score.

Redlining refers to a time when some financial institutions would literally draw a red line on a map around the minority neighborhoods in which they did not want to offer financial services. The Federal Community Reinvestment act was passed in 1977 to put an end to all redlining practices, at least in theory. If you want access to affordable credit, if you want the chance to get a mortgage, or a credit card, or a car loan you should live in a white neighborhood. A white person living in a black neighborhood has less access to affordable credit; a black person living in a white neighborhood has more access to affordable credit. Attending a black college can also lower your credit score. It is, of course, illegal to lower your credit score based upon skin color; it is apparently legal to lower your credit score if you are in the general proximity of a minority.

The credit bureaus receive about 90% of their revenue from the merchants that use their services, mainly banks. When a bank submits information to a credit reporting bureau, the information goes immediately on the credit report, even if the information is incorrect. Seventy-nine percent (79%) of the credit reports contained serious errors - false delinquencies or accounts that did not belong to the consumer - that could result in the denial of credit. Forty-one percent (41%) of the credit reports contained personal demographic identifying information that was misspelled, long-outdated, belonged to a stranger, or was otherwise incorrect. Twenty percent (20%) of the credit reports were missing major credit, loan, mortgage, or other consumer accounts that demonstrate the creditworthiness of the consumer. Twenty-six percent (26%) of the credit reports contained credit accounts that had been closed by the consumer but incorrectly remained listed as open. Altogether, 87% of the credit reports contained either serious errors or other mistakes of some kind.

If you want to correct errors on your credit report you will need the patience of Job. The credit bureaus use software that automatically rejects your request to correct errors. The burden of proof is on you, not the banks. The simple truth is that banks want you to have a low credit score because they can charge higher interest rates. Lower-income, single, and minority borrowers are also more likely to pay late fees. A 2006 Demos study reveals that households with incomes below $25,000 are twice as likely to pay credit card rates of more than 20% than those earning $50,000 and five times more likely to pay such rates than those earning $100,000.

Are lower income customers charged higher rates because they are more likely to default? No, higher rates, not lower income, are the primary cause of defaults.

Chapter 19

Payday Loans, Other Sharks, the Unbanked – The Modern Day Loan Sharks

If your credit score drops too far, the banks will have nothing to do with you. It is possible to fall off the credit score radar and that means no more credit cards, no more bank loans, and no more emergency net. More than 20 million Americans cash more than $60 billion in checks each year at check-cashing businesses. The Community Financial Services Association is the lobbying group for the payday lending industry and they describe their clients as "the heart of America's middle class". The check cashing/payday loan store first appeared in the 1990s and it grew faster than a cancer. There are now more than 22,000 payday loan stores, more US locations that McDonalds and Burger King combined.

The payday loan is structured as a trap. Say you need to borrow $100 for two weeks. Simply fill out a quick and easy application, show proof of employment, show I.D., give the names and phone numbers of a handful of friends, and write a bad check dated for the next payday, and be sure to tack on fees. You write a personal check for $115, with $15 the fee to borrow the money. The check casher or payday lender agrees to hold your check until your next payday. When that day comes around, the lender deposits the check and you redeem it by paying the $115 in cash; about 25% of the borrowers do exactly that. The rest get caught in the trap; they roll-over the loan and are charged $15 more to extend the financing for 14 more days. If you agree to electronic payments instead of a check, here's what would happen on your next payday: the company would debit the full amount of the loan from your checking account electronically, or extend the loan for an additional $15. The cost of the initial $100 loan is a $15 finance charge and an annual percentage rate of 390 percent. If you roll-over the loan three times, the finance charge would climb to $60 to borrow the $100 and the annual percentage rate can jump well above 1,000 percent. The profit margins are similar to conventional banking but based on millions of small transactions.

Some states have realized that payday lenders are just the latest incarnation of loan sharks. Fifteen states recently capped interest rates on short-term loans, or kicked out payday lenders altogether. So, more big banks are getting into the payday loan market. The state of Ohio has imposed a 28% interest rate limit on payday loans, but thanks to interstate commerce rules, nationally chartered banks don't have to follow local rules (remember the *Marquette* ruling from 1978). After Ohio limited rates, Cincinnati-based Fifth Third Bank, which has 400 branches in the state but also operates in 11 other states, introduced its Early Access Loan, with an annual interest rate of 120%. Fifth Third Bank and U.S. Bancorp started offering the loans. Wells Fargo continues to boost its payday loan program, which it began in 1994.

Payday loan companies figured out the idea of redlining almost immediately, but their version had nothing to do with discrimination against people based on skin color; they merely took a map and circled military bases. Military personnel fit the payday loan demographics: young and poorly paid.

The payday loan/check cashing business is so profitable that banks have gotten into the action with tax refund anticipation loans. When customers of tax preparation companies learn they have a tax refund coming, they are offered the chance to get the money almost immediately. For a fee, the tax preparer arranges a bank loan for the refund amount. The bank then keeps the refund when it arrives from the government.

IRS rules prevent tax preparation firms from directly granting the loans, so the tax firms partner with a third-party bank. H&R Block, the nation's largest tax preparation firm, works with HSBC Bank. More than one-third of Jackson Hewitt's revenue comes from refund anticipation loans. The tax refund loans general work out to more than 100% on an annualized rate, but the taxpayer can get the money in a matter of two or three days, as opposed to filing an electronic return and waiting 11 days for the government to send them a refund.

Perhaps the fastest growing segment of the population is the unbanked, somewhere between 30 to 70 million people who have no bank accounts. The unbanked include new immigrants, the poor, the unemployed, the blacklisted, and people who just stopped trusting banks and got tired of being ripped off. For some people, not using banks is a form of civil disobedience. Undocumented immigrants probably number around 12 million and many work on a cash only basis. The number of unemployed, part-time, or marginally attached workers has recently climbed to at least 26 million.

ChexSystems is a reporting agency which compiles a report of everything that your banks have reported in your last 5 years of banking. But unlike credit reports, ChexSystems reports only contain negative information, such as bounced checks, unpaid overdraft fees, charges, and unpaid lines of credit; there may be good reasons for this activity and there may be good history to offset the transgressions, but it is not reported. The banks can even close your account if you make too many deposits that bounce – even though you are the victim of the bounced check. Once someone gets listed on Chex it can be tough to open a new bank account; they are effectively blacklisted. The exact number of the blacklisted is proprietary information, but believed to be in the millions. The typical unbanked person has an average household income of $27,000; most are married, have at least one child, and are employed by a small business.

Many people just don't trust banks. Just because someone is unbanked doesn't mean the usurers won't extract a pound of flesh. Over a lifetime, the average full-time, unbanked worker will spend more than $40,000 just to turn his or her salary into cash, or approximately 1 ½ years of work just to collect their pay.

The banks have invaded the US economy like parasites, sucking out their take from almost all pay checks and then taking more when the money is spent. The rates charged are usurious in the extreme. The old debates about reasonable versus excessive interest rates have vanished. Once the limits were removed, the banks could gorge like swollen ticks. And still they wanted more. There are limits to consumer spending and consumer debt. People can only buy so many basics; you only eat a certain amount of food; you only buy enough soap to use over the next few weeks or months.

Chapter 20

The Housing Bubble – After Stealing Everything Else the Bankers Target Your Home

The next bubble came from housing, and although there are limits on the number of houses a family might realistically consider buying, usually one per family, many families were not at that limit. One answer was to bring more buyers into the market, and another more powerful approach was to create feverish speculation in housing, also known as churning or flipping.

Street criminals do not hang out to rob people coming out of the gym or the shooting range. The banks did not push their sub-prime loans outside the shareholder convention of Warren Buffet's Berkshire Hathaway. The Community Reinvestment Act of 1977 (CRA) was intended to prevent the practice of redlining and make affordable mortgages available to more people. CRA was not the cause of the subprime crisis that would hit the banks and the economy in 2006; nearly 60% of higher-priced loans went to middle- or higher-income borrowers, or neighborhoods outside of the scope of CRA lending. Additionally, the 20% of subprime loans that did go to low- or moderate-income areas or borrowers were originated by nonbank lenders not covered by CRA obligations. Only 6% of all higher-priced loans were made by CRA-covered lenders to borrowers and neighborhoods protected by the CRA.

Laws were rewritten to prevent state attorneys general from enforcing lending laws. The argument was that stopping predatory lending practices would deny minorities the chance to achieve home ownership. They preyed on minorities with a vengeance. African American and Hispanic borrowers were 450% more likely than whites to get stuck with predatory loans. One loan officer would later testify: "If someone appeared uneducated, inarticulate, was a minority, or was particularly old or young, I would try to include all the [additional costs] CitiFinancial offered."

Various studies indicate that up to 40% of those who were sold excessive interest rate mortgages could have qualified for lower interest rate, traditional mortgages; the banks knew this and they took advantage of their customers anyway. The banks were predators, pure and simple. Low income, middle income, and even upper income families were all targeted if they appeared vulnerable. In 2009, the Center for Responsible Lending testified in Congress regarding deceptive lending practices, specifically a form of mortgage broker compensation called "yield premium spread". The CRL is a non-partisan organization focused on consumer protection. The YSP was an extra payment - a kickback - that brokers received for delivering a mortgage with a higher interest rate than one for which the borrower would usually qualify. The yield spread premiums typically encouraged brokers to offer "no doc" loans even when borrowers could verify their income, but also generally required the mortgage to have a prepayment penalty. Many of these non-standard mortgages (Alt-A, Option-ARM) were written during the late stages of the housing bubble. These are precisely the mortgages that will continue to be reset into 2012. And there is a mountain of them.

In September 2007, the CRL testified to Congress about the wave of coming subprime foreclosures, encouraging Congress to act before the crisis escalated. "As it turned out," the CRL noted in its later testimony, "our predictions – dismissed by some as pessimistic – actually underestimated the dimensions of the crisis." There is no doubt that in the early 2000s there were predatory subprime loans made, and those loans were made in neighborhoods that had once been redlined, but this was not enough to set up a bubble; this was not enough activity to pull the entire economy out of a post 9/11 recession.

With Federal Reserve discount interest rates near 1 percent, the bankers were literally swamped with money. They started lending to people who already owned homes. For many people, refinancing was an opportunity to pay down other debts, but for most it was more like installing an ATM at the front door. Home Equity Lines of Credit (HELOC) and second mortgages were touted as an easy way to buy a car or a flat screen TV. Bankers advertised that homeowners could tap into your equity! Countrywide, one of the largest subprime lenders sent out up to 8 million targeted mailers per month between 2004 and 2006, urging people who typically had debt problems to refinance. Since the early 1980s, the value of home equity loans outstanding has ballooned from $1 billion to more than $1 trillion. Nearly a quarter of Americans with first mortgages now have a HELOC, as well. Banks' returns on fixed-rate home equity loans and lines of credit, which are the most popular, are 25 percent to 50 percent higher than returns on consumer loans over all, with much of that premium coming from relatively high fees. For the first time since World War II, the portion of home value that Americans own has fallen to less than 50 percent; in the 1980s, that figure was 70 percent, and negative equity is at historic highs. Banks were siphoning equity.

Used car sellers have an old trick; they divert the buyer's attention from the price of the car and direct the attention to the monthly payments. "If I can get your payments down to just $199 a month, would you drive that beauty home today?" A few years later, the car would break down and the buyer would return to the used car dealer only to learn they still owed more on the car than the current trade-in value; they were underwater. No problem, the old loan was rolled over into a new loan and the buyer went deeper and deeper into debt; a trick later picked up by payday loan shysters, but there are limits to the number of rollovers, and eventually the buyer is left with a clunker and a big debt.

The Federal Reserve and the predatory mortgage lenders learned the first trick; they lowered the monthly payments. The Fed cut interest rates. The banks wrote mortgages with introductory teaser rates to give the appearance of passing along those low rates. Demand for houses increased; inventories of homes for sale decreased, and prices for homes shot up. In 2004, houses were offered for sale and sold in one day, and then resold a week later. Interest rates slowly inched higher from the post 9/11 lows. To compensate for higher homes prices and higher interest rates, lenders created "Neg Am" or negative amortization loans, meaning the initial rate was so low that the monthly payments didn't lower the mortgage, but added more debt. Lenders sold the exotic mortgages on the idea that home prices would continue to go up, up, and away. Buyers went along for the dream; after all, home prices nearly doubled from 2001 to 2006. Many borrowers thought the low rates established by the Federal Reserve were being passed to them; they didn't realize they were holding a ticking debt bomb.

The housing market was churning. Buyers dreamed of making a 10% down payment on a $200,000 home, adding granite countertops and selling for $400,000. The lenders dreamed that prices would continue to climb and the mortgage churning would continue. The bankers make money on every mortgage originated. One economist described the market as a form of delusion. Mass delusion only goes so far in explaining the problem; at the root was a familiar sin – usury.

Chapter 21

What is a Fair Price? – Is a 5,000% Markup Reasonable?

Manufacturers calculate cost of goods, overhead, sales expense and evaluate the market to determine a fair price. Retailers of non-perishable goods generally mark up wholesale prices 100% for resale. The most successful retailers have been those that discounted this formula. Perishable goods like fruits, vegetables and meat is generally marked up 3 times the cost to cover spoilage and still cover overhead and marketing expense. Usury laws, prior to 1978, outlawed "loan shark" rates and helped establish fair pricing. We have the same type laws to protect consumers from profiteering at times of natural disasters. It is unconscionable to go to an area that was devastated by tornado, hurricane or earthquake and sell a bottle of water for $20. California sets its usury law at 10% or 5% above the Federal Reserve Bank rate, whichever is greater. This takes into account "cost of goods" and enough to cover expenses and a fair profit. Banks (as of the time of this writing) can borrow money from the Federal Reserve at 0.5%. They then loan the money on credit cards at 25% plus - that equates to a 5000% mark-up. A 10% mortgage loan is a 2000% mark-up over the cost of goods. That makes the $20 bottle of water look cheap.

The basic formula for a mortgage was that a buyer would take out a $100,000 mortgage on a home and the buyer would pay approximately $239,000 (at 7%) over the term of the prime 30 year mortgage. The buyer would pay for the house in 13 years and pay for the bankers for 17 years (the banker was paid first). The bankers never drove a nail, never laid a block or tile or shingle, and for this they would receive four times the money that was paid to the builder. The arrangement did not provide much value for the buyer until inflation and tax deductions were figured into the equation. When limits on usury were removed, the bankers jacked up rates wherever they could get away with it; first on subprime borrowers, then on anybody they could pillage (Alt-A or no documentation loans), and the value to the buyer dropped. The same $100,000 mortgage for a subprime borrower might cost $484,000 over a 30 year mortgage. The subprime borrower was on the hook for $245,000 more than the prime borrower; nearly a quarter of a million dollars that could have put kids through college, bought new cars, or been a nest egg for retirement. The majority of subprime borrowers were middle class families just hoping for the American Dream of home ownership. The bankers tricked many of these borrowers into paying nearly five times the sales price. Is it any wonder there were so many defaults?

Why did so many families get stuck with excessively high rate mortgages? The answer is asymmetrical information, a theory developed by Nobel Prize winning economist Joseph Stiglitz. In any transaction one party has more information than the other party to the transaction, and the party that has more information ends up with the better terms. Or, very simply – if you know more than the other guy you get the best deal. The mortgage lenders had lawyers to draft the contracts, accountants to calculate the terms, and brokers to hustle up lenders. On the other side of the table a plumber, nurse, cop, or soldier was handed a stack of papers two inches thick and a title officer would tell them where to sign. For many buyers it was their first chance to look at the paperwork. Good Faith Estimates and Truth in Lending documents were frequently different than the pile of documents that was plopped down on the table at closing.

Angelo Mozilo, then CEO of Countrywide Financial, the largest mortgage lender sent emails acknowledging the problem: Loans had been originated: "through our channels with disregard for process [and] compliance with guidelines." He "personally observed a serious lack of compliance within our origination system". Apparently Mozilo took no significant action to protect consumers. Forensic audits would later reveal that 83% of mortgages contained serious violations of lending laws, but that was only revealed after the fact.

Why did the banks abuse their customers in this way? The answer is the same answer that murders and thieves and rapists have given over the ages; they did it because they could.

In the summer of 2006, the bubble started to deflate and house prices slipped. Adjustable rate mortgages reset, balloon payments came due, and monthly payments jumped higher. Like the used car buyer that was only concerned with monthly payments, the borrowers discovered they owed more than the home was worth, they were underwater. Most homeowners did everything they could to keep making payments; they dipped into their savings if they had any, and when savings ran out they turned to their plastic, rolling over the debt into a bigger debt.

The bankers claimed the interest rate they were charging was to compensate for the risk they were taking in extending credit to lower tiered borrowers. This was before the Federal Bailout where they assumed none of the risk, but kept all the prior profits. An amazing statistic emerges when default rates are calculated on adjustable rate loans. Loans that started with a 1% "teaser rate" had a minimal default rate that was insignificantly different from prime borrowers. When the interest rate was adjusted slightly higher, to a rate that was comparable to a prime loan, the rate of default was still within the norm. When rates were increased to excessive, usurious, predatory levels, the defaults skyrocketed. Therefore, the increased risk of default can be attributed to only one thing, the greed of the bankers and usurious rates. If rates had stayed at 5-5½ % (0.5% + 5% over the cost of funds) the risk of default would have been greatly reduced. The risk was not because the borrowers had a low credit score; the risk came from the bankers charging predatory rates. Mark Twain said, "I am more concerned with the return of my money than the return on my money". The bankers had a far greater chance of receiving a return of the principal if they had only charged a fair, non-usurious rate on that loan, and our national financial crisis may have been averted. The greatest risk in lending is the bankers' greed.

Chapter 22

Why Loan Mods Don't Work – The Banks Bet Against the Homeowners

While it would have made sense for the bankers to voluntarily reduce the interest rates on the sub-prime loans to below usury rates and have the homeowners continue to make payments, greed and Credit Default Swaps got in the way.

The homeowners called the bankers and begged for mercy. In 2007, at a convention of mortgage brokers, one broker told of fielding a call from a desperate homeowner hoping to modify a predatory loan. The homeowner had been transferred and disconnected multiple times. The broker said he would transfer the caller to the department that could help - department 32. The room erupted in laughter. When the broker went home for the night the phone line was still blinking, the homeowner was still waiting patiently to talk with someone in department 32. Again the convention room broke out in nervous laughter. The assembled brokers all knew the inside joke – there was no department 32.

Another man sent an email to Countrywide, politely begging for some break so he could stay in his home of 16 years. The reply came directly from Angelo Mozilo, former CEO of Countrywide. Mozilo knew the predatory tactics of his company and still he wrote an email calling the plea for help "Disgusting." Instead of hitting reply, Mozilo forwarded the email to the Los Angeles Times.

Banks that are capable of tracking the purchase of a cup of coffee in Moscow or Manhattan – down to the penny, became completely incompetent when it came to modifying mortgages. Paperwork was lost, faxes were never received, and loan modification applications were lost and lost again and again. Despite all the violations of lending laws, the banks were never forced to accountability. Enforcement of lending laws remains lax. Loan modifications remain voluntary. There were no new laws enacted to stop foreclosures – none.

Complicating the process, the originating lender is often not the servicing agent of a mortgage. Payment from the homeowner and to investors who are the ultimate owners of the security (mortgage backed security – MBS, collateralized mortgage obligation – CMO, and collateralized debt obligation – CDO) is handled by a mortgage servicer who collects a fee for its work. There is considerable distance between the homeowner and the ultimate holder of the mortgage note. There is a byzantine web of originating bank, mortgage holder, mortgage servicer, MBS pooling/securitizing agent, and investors. The homeowner doesn't have a clue who to call in order to get relief to avoid foreclosure.

The National Consumer Law Center issued a research paper claiming: "Once a mortgage loan is made, in most cases the original lender does not have further ongoing contact with the homeowner. Instead, the original lender, or the investment trust to which the loan is sold, hires a servicer to collect monthly payments. It is the servicer that either answers the borrower's plea for a modification or launches a foreclosure. Servicers spend millions of dollars advertising their concern for the plight of homeowners and their willingness to make deals. Yet the experience of many homeowners and their advocates is that servicers—not the mortgage owners—are often the barrier to making a loan modification." The largest loan servicers are Bank of America, Wells Fargo, JP Morgan Chase, and CitiMortgage.

Why don't servicers make loan mods? Follow the money. Servicers make money from monthly servicing fees; a fixed percentage of the unpaid principal balance of the loans in the pool, and from fees charged borrowers in default, including late fees, process management fees, and other junk fees. Servicers lose no money from foreclosures because they recover all of their expenses when a loan is foreclosed, before any of the investors get paid. The rules for recovery of expenses in a modification are much less clear and somewhat less generous. Also, since the servicers don't hold the mortgage note, they don't make the ultimate decision to modify or foreclose. It is fairly easy to drag out a foreclosure; it is extremely difficult to get a concessionary modification.

The bankers and investors prefer a foreclosure because they can collect the Credit Default Swap "insurance" payments on defaults. A loan modification is not considered a default and does not trigger an insurance payout. Foreclosures and short sales are considered defaults. The bankers were betting the mortgages would default. They didn't care whether they modified a loan for the homeowner; they were only interested in collecting the insurance. The bankers were betting against the homeowner.

With each foreclosure, the price of all homes started to drop. By 2009, more than one quarter of all homes with mortgages were underwater, the mortgage was more than the current market value of the property. It is estimated that half of all homes with mortgages will be underwater by the end of 2011. More than one quarter of all homeowners intentionally stop making mortgage payments; that number is expected to grow to 50% or more – in line with the number of mortgages with negative equity. People are just trying to escape the debt. It's called Strategic Default.

Here's how the strategy works: a homeowner with a $400,000 mortgage realizes that the current market value of the house is only $200,000. They realize that paying for that $200k in negative equity over the life of a 30 year mortgage will actually cost from $480,000 to $800,000, depending on rates (for most people that is their retirement nest egg). They also realize that they can go down the street and buy a comparable home for $200,000 in the name of the spouse, or with cash, or with hard money loans from family or friends, or they can just rent for a few years while they flood the credit bureaus with letters to clean their credit. They can stop making payments and still live in the current house for 3 months to one year before they are evicted. They are aware that the mortgage is a nonrecourse loan, meaning the bank gets the house, but can't go after the borrower's other assets. The borrower loses their equity and gets hit with lower credit scores. The bank gets the house. That was the deal going in.

Chapter 23

Foreclosure and the Courts – How Your Legal Protection Was Stolen & the Fight for Justice

Federal Bankruptcy judges, like all Federal judges, have lifetime appointments. They are considered some of our best legal minds. Prior to 2005, Bankruptcy judges had a great deal of discretion in deciding what could be done in bankruptcy court. The banks pushed through legislation in 2005 that made bankruptcy much more difficult. Is it a coincidence that credit card companies were carrying the highest balances in history? Is it a coincidence that 2005 was the final wave of sub-prime loans? Did the banks know that usury creates higher defaults and they were getting ready to be hit with a tsunami of defaults? Industry lobbyists hand crafted changes to the bankruptcy code that made charge offs harder and forced most borrowers into Chapter 13 repayment plans, rather than Chapter 7, which writes off the debt and gives the filer a fresh start. The Corporatist politicians dutifully passed the law.

The change in the bankruptcy laws had some unusual consequences. Bankruptcy filings hit a record high of over 2 million in 2005 as people rushed to get in under the deadline. Filing for bankruptcy became more of an ordeal, but not impossible. The bankruptcy rate dropped significantly in 2006, but started climbing again in 2007 – up 40%, and jumped nearly 25%, to over one million in 2008, then jumped 40% in 2009. Making it tougher to file bankruptcy did not result in fewer bankruptcies.

The typical bankrupt filer is in their 30s, likely to be female (53.8% v. 46.2% male), two-thirds are employed. Beyond that the demographics tend to be subjective. According to one survey the major reason for bankruptcies was medically related, 62%, even though three-quarters of those medically related bankruptcy applicants had health insurance. Overextended on credit, unexpected expenses, and reduction of income are all cited as major reasons for filing bankruptcy. Of course illness/injury can lead to reduction of income, unexpected expenses and overextension of credit.

Another reason that is never cited is bankers' greed. When bankers charge excessive interest rates and fees, they increase the probability of default. A borrower who is treated fairly and honestly is more likely to do everything they can to repay their debt. A borrower who gets screwed by the bankers is more likely to tell the bankers to go to hell.

Bankruptcy judges have broad discretion to force creditors to modify the terms of loans, but the discretion to modify home mortgages was stripped away in 2005 with the new bankruptcy laws. The judges were no longer in control. Foreclosures grew at a rate that had not been seen since the Great Depression.

The courts are not completely powerless. A few enlightened judges have been standing up to the bankers; understandably, there has been almost no media coverage of the legal battles against illegal foreclosures. When the bankers were writing mortgages and then selling them off in securitized bundles, they forgot a minor detail – they forgot to hold onto the note.

A man walks into a bank and says he'd like to cash a check. The teller says, "Very good. May I see the check?"

The man says, "I don't have it. I sold the check to hedge fund in the Cayman Islands. The fund sold it to other investors; they split the cash flow from the check and sold that to still other investors. I'm not sure where the check is now but I can assure you that I am the rightful holder of the check."

The teller says, "That's very nice. When you are rightfully holding the check in front of me I'll be glad to assist you in your transaction."

The man returns the next day and says he'd like to cash a check. The teller says, "Very good. May I see the check?"

The man says, "I don't have it, but I'm a very clever fellow. Before I sold the check to the hedge fund in the Cayman Islands, I gave the check to a company that makes an electronic copy of the check. They have sent me a copy of their copy. I still don't know where the original check is. It could be anywhere in the world by now, but I'd like to get cash for the copy of the copy of the check. As you can clearly see, the copy has my name on it."

As incredible as it may seem, this is the tactic of banks trying to foreclose on homeowners. The mortgage note and the check are essentially promises to pay, or promissory notes. One of the key elements in trying to collect on a promissory note is to show that you rightfully hold the note. The dirty little secret is that the banks do not rightfully hold the notes on approximately 60 million mortgages; the reason they do not hold the notes is because they sold the notes; before they sold the notes, they made copies with a company called MERS (Mortgage Electronic Registration System). Servicers disregard that banks sold the notes and try to foreclose, in violation of the Fair Debt Collections Practices Act.

There have been several judges that have displayed the wisdom to see through the bankers scam. MERS is a private company that registers mortgages electronically and tracks changes in ownership; if you don't pay your mortgage then MERS will foreclose. The Kansas Supreme Court says MERS is nothing but a "straw man" and they have no standing to foreclose. In *Landmark National Bank v. Kesler*, the Kansas Supreme Court held that nominee company MERS has no right or legal standing to bring action for foreclosure.

The securitization of mortgages meant that the mortgage loan was chopped into pieces and sold off to investors, bundled together with other mortgage loans to create Mortgage Backed Securities (MBS), and the income stream was bundled into Collateralized Mortgage Obligations (CMO) or Collateralized Loan Obligations (CLO) or Collateralized Debt Obligations (CDO). These financial products were then "insured" with Credit Default Swaps (CDS). These derivative financial products were <u>sold</u> to pension funds, hedge funds, foreign investment funds, offshore units of banks (for tax evasion purposes), and other investors. There were many parties who bought these derivative financial products that were presumed to be backed by mortgage loans secured by real property.

MERS supposedly kept track of all these changes electronically – at least that was the theory. The reality is that MERS would register and record the mortgage loans in its name. To have tracked all the parties in the derivative financial products would have been like making apples out of apple sauce. And if homeowners missed their payments, MERS would bring foreclosure action in its name. Did MERS hold the promissory note? No, it just copied the note electronically, and did a poor job at that. The MERS website says: "MERS is an innovative process that simplifies the way mortgage ownership and servicing rights are originated, sold and tracked. Created by the real estate finance industry, MERS eliminates the need to prepare and record assignments when trading residential and commercial mortgage loans." Sounds good but it is illegal.

The originating lender has no standing to foreclose once he sells off the mortgage. He was paid in full and thus has no standing to appear in court. And since he was paid in full he can't demand payment again. Can just anybody force collection on a promissory note? Try walking into a bank and asking them to cash a check. You have to have a real check in your hand to cash the check. Why?

Because if they pay you, the real holder of the check may walk in with the actual check and demand payment – and they don't want to pay twice. MERS tried to force collection on promissory notes, but the notes were nowhere to be found.

Another problem: MERS not only facilitated the rapid turnover of mortgages and mortgage-backed securities, but it has served as a sort of corporate veil that protects investors from claims by borrowers concerning predatory lending practices. This cast a dark pall over transparency. Homeowners could no longer identify the true holder of their note. MERS would foreclose even though they had no financial interest in the property – just being a nominee and tracking agent did not make MERS the holder in due course of the promissory note. The problem is that the securitization process cut off the homeowners' ability to due process with respect to discovery of the origination and servicing and payment of predatory loans that may have been chock full of lending violations. Any discovery ends with the proxy MERS. The real holder of the note? Who knows? MERS doesn't know. And there is a good chance the real holder doesn't really want to step forward and be exposed to tax evasion charges for funneling the cash flow from the security conduits into offshore tax havens. The Kansas Supreme Court stated that MERS' relationship "is more akin to that of a straw man than to a party possessing all the rights given a buyer."

MERS as straw man lacks standing to foreclose, but so does the original lender, although it was a signatory to the deal. The lender lacks standing because title had to pass to the secured parties for the arrangement to legally qualify as a security. The lender has been paid in full and has no further legal interest in the claim. Only the securities holders have skin in the game; but they have no standing to foreclose, because they were not signatories to the original agreement. They cannot satisfy the basic requirement of contract law that a plaintiff suing on a written contract must produce a signed contract proving he is entitled to relief.

The pretender lenders are gaming the system every day and literally stealing homes from both homeowners and investors who thought they had an interest in those homes when they bought mortgage backed securities. This leaves the borrower in a position of financial double jeopardy wherein the true owner of the loan can still make a claim and the investor is simply out of luck because they have been misinformed about the payments or status of the pool of assets the investor bought into.

This is not the first time the holder in course of a note could not be found. In October 2007, U.S. District Court Judge Boyko ruled that Deutsche Bank had not filed the proper paperwork to establish its right as trustee to foreclose on 14 homes. Judge Boyko wrote: "The institutions seem to adopt the attitude that since they have been doing this for so long, unchallenged, this practice equates with legal compliance. Finally put to the test, their weak legal arguments compel the Court to stop them at the gate."

A Massachusetts judge refused to reverse a ruling (*Ibanez*) that opens up the very real possibility that tens of thousands of foreclosures in the state, dating as far back as 1989, could be invalidated. The judge denied a request made by Wells Fargo and U.S. Bank to reinstate two foreclosures that he had invalidated in 2009 because the lenders did not hold clear title to them at the time of the foreclosure sale.

In a 27-page ruling, Justice Keith C. Long described a convoluted process in which mortgages for the two homes were transferred multiple times without being properly recorded, as required by state foreclosure law. He said any problems the banks now face to clean up title questions – which could include redoing the foreclosures altogether – are "entirely of their own making."

In his decision, Judge Long stated: "The issues in this case are not merely problems with paperwork or a matter of dotting i's and crossing t's. Instead, they lie at the heart of the protections given to homeowners and borrowers by the Massachusetts legislature. To accept the plaintiffs' arguments is to allow them to take someone's home without any demonstrable right to do so, based upon the assumption that they ultimately will be able to show that they have that right and the further assumption that potential bidders will be undeterred by the lack of a demonstrable legal foundation for the sale and will nonetheless bid full value in the expectation that that foundation will ultimately be produced, even if it takes a year or more. The law recognizes the troubling nature of these assumptions, the harm caused if those assumptions prove erroneous, and commands otherwise."

For now, banks continue to steal homes. Only a few judges are willing to stand up to the bankers. Again, usury refers to any gain on a loan. Selling a mortgage note to investors and then coming back to foreclose on the mortgage qualifies as excessive usury.

Section Four

The Inflationary, Bloodsucking, Cancerous, Enslaving, Catastrophic Economics of Usury

Chapter 24

Usury and Inflation – Usury Creates Inflation

Back to basics. Money is a medium of exchange. Some of the earliest forms of money were precious metals, gold and silver, mainly because it was rare (as opposed to any old stone). Coins made of gold or silver were certainly easier to exchange than a goat, or a boat, or cheese. Gold and silver coins did not rot or rust or die or turn putrid – unlike boats, goats, or cheese – and so the coins became a store of value. Money was used as a receipt to acknowledge the value received in a transaction. Government minted coins to correspond to the goods or services produced – until usury.

If a man borrowed 100 coins he would have to repay 110 coins (at 10% interest) at the end of the year. Where did the extra 10 coins come from? If the borrower was able to produce 10% more, the coins were minted to reflect the production and the lender received the extra production.

If the borrower did not increase production, the coins were still minted, but there was no production to back the coins; the money supply was artificially inflated. All money held less value. The purchasing power decreased. If the interest rate on the loan exceeds the increase in production, the result is inflation. It makes no difference if we are talking about gold coins or digital entries on a computer. The only reasons to increase money supply are to match the economic growth from increased production (this does not cause inflation), or to match the increase from debt (this causes inflation).

The Federal Reserve creates money by increasing debt. The government issues bonds and the money is created by the Federal Reserve to purchase the bonds. It really is that simple – the Federal Reserve creates money out of thin air. Interest taken on debt does not represent value for goods produced. Most of the money in circulation is not printed or minted, but digitally added to the money supply to correspond to the increase in credit. The banks add money to circulation by making more loans. The result is too much money chasing too few goods. Each coin, each dollar, each measurement of money in circulation holds less value. Usury causes inflation.

If the money supply only increased as much as production increased, there would be no inflation (absent devaluation of the currency). If debt is used to produce goods or services (think of a business loan to buy equipment), the increase in production can offset the inflation created by usury. It is rare that the increase in production is as high as the rate of interest charged on debt. If the usury rate is in excess of the increase in production the result is inflation. Debt that is not used to produce something, merely consumer debt, results in even more inflation.

Consumer debt is literally robbing future production; it is borrowing from the future to pay for the present. The era of ever-increasing debt hasn't benefited the borrowers who got buried under debt to buy things they couldn't afford. The beneficiaries were the big banks, JPMorgan Chase, Bank of America, Citicorp, and Wells Fargo. The 10 biggest US banks now control more than 50% of all deposits in the nation, more than 50% of the mortgage market, and 88% of the credit card market. They no longer compete to earn a customer's business; they sweep up the smaller bank failures and the Treasury Department and the Federal Reserve insure them against failure.

The increase in the money supply does not increase the wealth of people or of nations. Money is still a store of value. Simply by putting more money in circulation, each unit of money is worth less; each unit of money stores less value. Think of money as receipts for coins; for example if you have 100 ounces of silver and you issue 100 pieces of paper to represent that stored silver, each piece of paper is worth one ounce of silver. If you issue 200 pieces of paper, each piece of paper is worth one-half ounce of silver. Issuing twice as many pieces of paper does not make the silver double in weight.

Likewise, when a bank lends $100 dollars at 10% interest the borrower must increase their productive output by 10% or inflation will occur. Let's use the example of silver coins again: 100 silver coins are loaned at 10%; production increases 10% - no inflation. If the borrower increases production by only 5%, the value of money in circulation will be diluted by 5% - that is inflation. Nobody likes inflation. For the lender who lends $100 dollars at 10% all of his profits will be lost if the inflation rate is 10%. At the end of the year he has $110 dollars but he only has the buying power of $100. The borrower must produce 10% more just to repay the loan and the interest. If the borrower wants to make a profit, he must increase production by more than 10%.

The lender has done nothing to earn his 10%; he has not added value to his community. In this way usury oppresses the poor. The national economy is really pretty similar to a household economy. When every member of a household is able and does their part to support the family's comfort, the burden is equally distributed. If one member of the family can't perform their duties, the rest of the family must pick up the slack. When each member of a community contributes his or her portion to the common welfare, the burdens are equally distributed. When any one fails to contribute, the burdens are heavier for the rest of the community. Usury makes it possible for many to live on the incomes from their assets - they are not personally productive. This makes it necessary for the workers to produce more to provide the basic necessities of the community. The non-productive usurers also tend to be among the most active consumers; they make heavy drafts on the energies of others. The world does not grow richer, nor are the conditions of life for one class eased, by the extravagance of another class.

Some people claim that the idleness and extravagant lifestyles of a few may benefit others because they make a demand for more work. If a house is burning we don't tell the fire fighters to sit idly and let the house burn down because it might make more work for carpenters, plumbers, and electricians; this is not the way to house the homeless. Extravagance is simply wasteful destruction of property. While we have seen negative consequences of overconsumption, the world has never experienced the positive effects of overproduction. There can never be an oversupply of food, clean water, clothes, and shelter until all the needs of the poorest are supplied. The collection of usury restrains a large number of people from active production. Usury demands payment and if payment is not made, then shops, factories, fields, and warehouses are idled. Supply is restrained in order to extract a satisfactory increase on the property.

The collection of usury imposes a burden on all parties, even those who are not part of the specific transaction. Even if the borrower and lender agree to terms, and the terms are determined to be fair and reasonable, the ultimate result is that someone else will pay the profits to both lender and borrower. The tenants of the borrower ultimately pay the interest and the principle. A loan is made to a manufacturer and the interest is paid by all who buy the manufactured goods. A loan is made to a merchant and he collects from his customers. Usury oppresses the poor by raising the price of everything he consumes.

Our daily bread comes from wheat grown on mortgaged farmland and the interest is part of the price of wheat. The mill that processes wheat into flour is mortgaged and interest increases the cost of flour. The trucking firm that transports the flour has loans and bonds; the price goes up some more. The baker has loans and a mortgage, and those costs are wrapped into the loaf of bread. Usury takes a slice out of each loaf of bread, from the farm, to the mill, to the baker, and we pay for a full loaf, but we get less. Usury causes inflation.

Usury is charged to every person for every basic need, even if they personally avoid indebtedness. And as prices have gone perpetually higher, wages have stalled or dropped. Capital is employed first, labor is employed second. If labor can be eliminated by borrowing more capital, then a loan is secured and the worker dismissed. If cheaper labor can be found overseas, the local worker is dismissed. The usury must be paid first and if it is not, the enterprise is closed down. The opportunities for labor dry up, competition for jobs increases, and wages drop even more. Usury demands support and a continuous increase. For this reason unions and labor groups have never been able to win in a battle against capital. So long as capital has earning power, the owners of capital will demand that capital receives payment first, and receives the largest portion.

If inflation, which is cause by usury, increases significantly faster than economic growth, the result is hyper-inflation. We have seen economies that have experienced hyper-inflation, where it takes a wheelbarrow full of paper notes to buy a loaf of bread. When hyper-inflation happens, money stops being an effective medium of exchange and commerce grinds to a halt.

Chapter 25

Compounding – Exponential Increase: Debt Grows Like a Cancer

Any inflation is unsustainable because inflation, like interest charged, is compounded and grows exponentially. The formula for compounding is known as the Rule of 72's. The rule says that to find the number of years required to double money at a given interest rate, you just divide the interest rate into 72. For example, if you want to know how long it will take to double money at eight percent interest, divide 8 into 72 and get 9 years. Debt of $100 at 8% interest grows to $200 in 9 years, and $400 in 18 years, and $800 in 27 years. If one penny had been loaned at 8% interest in the year 1 A.D., then by the year 2010 the amount due would be:

$151,966,733,600,974,000,000,000,000,000,000,000,000,000,000,000,000,000,000,000,000,000.00

I'm not even sure what to call a number that large, but to give it some scale, if you took that money and bought gold at $1,000 per ounce you would have enough gold to make huge balls of gold the size of the earth, and you could then stack these golden planets one on top of the other and they would stretch out far beyond our solar system.

Still too big to wrap your brain around it? Try this; the US has about 300 million people; if each person borrowed $100 for 30 years (that's a total of $30 billion) at 8% compounded interest, at the end of 30 years we would owe $301,879,706,672.00 (>$301 billion).

Now for something a little closer to reality; total revolving credit card debt in 2009 was right at $931 billion; if interest is compounded at 14% over 10 years, the amount owed would be $3,451,423,043,444.39 (>$3 trillion). That's just credit card debt, not including mortgages, business debt, and governmental debt.

The point is that debt is unsustainable. As long as usury and the resulting inflation are allowed to exist, the only way to absorb the constant loss of buying power is to increase economic growth. This is a losing game. There are limits on economic growth and consumption. Most people in America already have shelter, food, clothing, and transportation. Most people don't want or need 10 houses or a new car every few months; they couldn't afford the purchases, or the effort and expense of maintenance. So, why is consumerism promoted with an evangelical fervor? We must feed the insatiable usury of the bankers.

The annual advertising budget in the US tops $280 billion and that's just traditional media advertising. There are billions more spent on subtle exhortations, displays, and enticements. The business of America has become fabricating desires rather than producing necessary goods and services. The most frequent topic of conversation in America is shopping; what we buy, where we buy, when we buy, and allegiances to purchases made or planned; this is considered valuable information and an important part of communication with strangers and loved ones. We are constantly bombarded with the message that spending will provide satisfaction and inner fulfillment. If you want to feel better, go shopping. To find love you need to spend lavishly. Shop till you drop. We are taught at an early age to seek the lifestyles of the rich and famous, despite the fact that many of the rich and famous are neurotic and unhappy. Business schools teach techniques for marketing to toddlers and teens. Americans, led by the Baby Boomers, have been living like spoiled children for 30 years. In many ways, we allowed the corporations to market to us as if we were children, with instant self-gratification as a major aspiration.

Most Americans took on significant amounts of debt not just because they wanted to, but because they had to. The reality is cold and simple. The American worker is still a whirlwind of productivity. Despite the increase in two-income families, wages have been stagnant for thirty years. The cost of goods and services, especially basic or durable goods and services, like cars, education, housing, and healthcare has exploded – fuelled by inflation which is fuelled by usury. When your income isn't going up, borrowing becomes the least bad option. The result is an economy where the middle class lost. Americans had to borrow because they weren't part of a shared prosperity to begin with.

Corporations have become experts at extracting value, but not at creating it. Prosperity wasn't shared because corporations weren't built for sharing. Workers are considered a liability, at least by the unenlightened. Corporations were built to create value for shareholders and to maximize profits by any means necessary: through lobbying, monopoly power, cost cutting, or by grabbing trillions in bailouts. Capitalism has been very good at taking value from workers and redistributing it to shareholders, redistributing wealth from the poorest to the richest. For the worker busting his or her butt to provide for a family, debt seemed like the only option to avoid poverty. The idea was that if you work your butt off you should be able to make a decent living, and if you're not making it now, take on a little debt to bridge the gap, because the hard work will surely pay off down the road; it did pay off, but not for the productive worker.

Chapter 26

Economic Disparity – The Great Divide, The Great Danger

Economic disparity is nothing new. The rich get richer and the poor get poorer. Maybe it has always been that way, but the trend has gained momentum in the past 30 years. The top 200 wealthiest families in the world control more wealth than the bottom 4 billion. The United States is the most economically stratified society in the western world. In 1976, the top 10% held 49% of the wealth and the bottom 90% owned 51% of the wealth. Now, the top 1% control 95% of the financial wealth in America. The top .01%, or 14,000 American families, control 22.2% of wealth — the bottom 90%, or over 133 million families, hold just 4% of the nation's wealth, but that's not counting debt. Another way of looking at it, the top 10% hold all the wealth and the bottom 50% don't have any wealth – just debt.

Real median household income in the United States hit $50,303 in 2009, but that number is down slightly from 1999 when the median household income was $50,641 adjusted for inflation. Per capita net worth, adjusted for inflation and the national debt, has decreased by 23%. In the mid-1970s, the median household income was $45,305, based upon one-income per household. Dual incomes became the only way to make ends meet, but two people earning incomes did not mean incomes doubled.

Meanwhile, worker productivity grew at twice the rate of 1999, meaning workers continue to produce more in less time. It must be because we have such great management; the average US CEO annual pay compared to a minimum wage worker's is 821:1 whereas twenty years ago the ratio was 40:1. (Some estimates have an even wider ratio.)

Many people argue that the wealthy are the most vital source of economic prosperity for all. The argument is that the wealthy (also known as Plutonomists) have more disposable income than the poor (true); the wealthy pay more taxes (partially true); and the wealthy create jobs that employ the masses (partially true, but small businesses are still the chief driver of employment and account for more than 65% of all new jobs). The argument is known as trickledown economics. The wealthiest 1% control 95% of the wealth; trickledown suggests that the wealthiest are the source of all prosperity. Think of a cake cut into 20 pieces and there are 100 people who want to eat. One person eats 19 pieces of cake and 99 people split the last slice. This is not quite the formula that Jesus used to feed the multitude. The wealthy gorge and the masses get the crumbs, and we should be thankful for the crumbs because without the wealthy there would be no crumbs at all.

Trickledown economics/plutonomics has gone from theory to real life application, and in real life it has failed. Theoretically the wealthy should have enough spending power to fuel an economic recovery. Theoretically the wealthy should have enough capital and intellect and vision to create new industries and new jobs. In real life, capital remains frozen, new industries are not being created, jobs are being lost at the fastest rate since the Great Depression, and poverty is the new norm. The United States fights two wars. Back home military families were being evicted, quite literally tossed to the curb like trash. The Plutonomists get tax breaks. What happened to the crumbs?

In 2007, John Thain, then CEO of Merrill Lynch pulled in $87 million in executive compensation, not including $1.2 million in 2008 to remodel his executive offices with niceties that included a $35,000 gold plated commode and $5,000 for a mirror so he could primp. Merrill Lynch would collapse in 2008 and be acquired by Bank of America. By comparison, the median expected salary for a Private First Class in the Army is $20,322 per year (2009 rate). It takes 4,281 Privates First Class to match the pay of John Thain.

From 2003 to 2008, Richard Fuld raked in $354 million as CEO of Lehman Brothers. The paychecks stopped in 2008 when

Lehman folded. It takes the annual pay of 17, 420 Privates First Class to match the five year paycheck of Richard Fuld.

In the five years prior to running Countrywide Financial into the ground, Angelo Mozilo pocketed $391 million. It takes the annual pay of 19,240 Privates First Class to match the five year paycheck of Angelo Mozilo.

Lloyd Blankfein's known compensation as CEO of Goldman Sachs for 2007 was $54 million, equivalent to the annual pay of 2,657 Privates First Class. Goldman bought and securitized billions in subprime loans, made a market for subprime bonds, and then bet that people would lose their homes as they shorted the market in 2007. Goldman generated windfall profits; screwing homeowners was just a bonus, and their position on bonuses is well documented. Goldman Sachs paid out $12.1 billion in bonuses to its 30,522 employees in 2007, or more than $396,000 per employee, and that's above and beyond their regular salaries and benefits. That $12.1 billion would be enough to pay the annual salaries of 595,413 Privates First Class.

In 2007, the 20 highest paid fund managers earned an average of $675.5 million, or $13.15 billion for speculating with other people's money. That's enough to pay the salaries of 647,082 Privates First Class.

With just the bonuses (not the salaries) from Goldman Sachs and the salaries of the 20 top hedge fund managers, the US could pay for 1,242,505 Privates First Class, a force unequalled in the history of the world. Of course, the Army doesn't have nearly that many Privates. Still, the $25.25 billion in Goldman bonuses and hedge fund salaries would be enough to build 252,500 nice homes for $100,000 each, and provide living quarters for the military families we do have.

Once again our country and especially our politicians show that our priorities are in perfect harmony with the bankers, not in support of our brave men and women that fight for our freedom. Abraham Lincoln once feared the bankers at his rear more than he feared the Southern army that he faced. We should guard our flanks.

In 2008, the Organization for Economic Co-operation and Development reported poverty in the US, defined as households with an income below half of the median national salary, rose to 17% in the US, meaning about 51 million Americans live in poverty. And here's some information that will shock you: in 2004, a typical black family had an income that was 58 percent of a typical white family. In 1974, median black incomes were 63 percent of those of whites.

In 1963 Rev. Dr. Martin Luther King, Jr. delivered his famous "I Have a Dream" speech which included these words:

"In a sense we've come to our nation's capital to cash a check. When the architects of our republic wrote the magnificent words of the Constitution and the Declaration of Independence, they were signing a promissory note to which every American was to fall heir. This note was a promise that all men, yes, black men as well as white men, would be guaranteed the "unalienable Rights" of "Life, Liberty and the pursuit of Happiness." It is obvious today that America has defaulted on this promissory note, insofar as her citizens of color are concerned. Instead of honoring this sacred obligation, America has given the Negro people a bad check, a check which has come back marked "insufficient funds."

"But we refuse to believe that the bank of justice is bankrupt. We refuse to believe that there are insufficient funds in the great vaults of opportunity of this nation. And so, we've come to cash this check, a check that will give us upon demand the riches of freedom and the security of justice."

Four decades later, the check is still marked "insufficient funds". The bank of justice is bankrupt for blacks and whites, men and women. In 2009, women surpassed men in the number of jobs held in America but those jobs paid 77% of what men were paid; hardly a victory for women's rights. The question of women's capability to perform the jobs was not the question or the reason why women surpassed men in the number of jobs. The shift was not about equality, it was about low wages. If women cost less they get the jobs. The struggle is not really between men and women; most families are a combination of men and women, and for most middle class families, both parents need to hold jobs to make ends meet.

After World War II, the middle class grew as never before. There were still rich people and poor people, but the gap was not huge. Fifty years after the Great Depression, the wealth gap started to grow.

The past 30 years have seen the greatest redistribution of wealth in the history of the US, and the money went from the middle class to the Corporatist elites. The rich have been getting richer and the poor have been getting poorer, but not just the poor; the middle class, the upper middle class, and even the upper class have seen their wealth redistributed to the very wealthy. The super rich get richer and everybody else gets poorer. The increasing wealth gap coincided exactly with the lifting of limits on usury; this is not a coincidence.

Chapter 27

Taxes, Tax Evasion, and Progressive Taxation – The Tax System is Tilted Toward the Rich

Everyone hates taxes! It would be un-American to actually like to pay taxes. Most would agree that it is our patriotic duty to pay our fair share; render unto Caesar what is Caesar's. The problem is everyone has a different opinion of what their fair share should be.

Until 1913, the Constitution allowed the federal government to impose 3 kinds of taxes: direct levies (such as property taxes), excise taxes on products, and tariffs on imported items. The widely accepted belief of the day was that tariffs alone would be sufficient to support the federal government. States imposed a combination of tariffs and direct taxes, such as head taxes. In 1913, the Constitution was changed and income taxes were allowed by the federal government.

Taxes have always been a means of not only collecting enough income to operate, but to control the population for the benefit of the masses. Collecting tariffs on foreign imports meant that locally produced goods would have an economic advantage. Direct levies of alcohol were the first common tax to decrease consumption and raise revenues.

Anything that takes money out of the pockets of someone without direct receipt of either goods or services is a tax. Usury is a tax on the borrower in excess of the fair return on one's investment. Bankers do not have the authority to impose a direct tax, but their usury surely does take excess property, providing nothing in return, except control over the borrower.

The rich made well scripted sales pitches and lobbied for tax cuts. They had the money to influence. It is without question that the rich have benefited most from tax cuts for the wealthiest individuals and corporations. Nobel Prize winning economist Paul Krugman reported that in a 29 year period from 1970 to 1999, the average salary in America rose 10%. Meanwhile, a Congressional Budget Study showed that from 1979 to 1997 after-tax incomes of the top 1% of American families rose 157%. In addition to cuts on the upper end of the marginal tax rate, a big change came when the capital gains rate was cut to 15%. For many of the wealthiest individuals, capital gains and dividends are a major source of income, and that income is taxed at a far lower rate than most middle class workers.

American-based multinational companies pay more of their income in foreign taxes than in domestic taxes; many try to avoid taxes altogether. According to a Government Accountability Office report, Bank of America, Citigroup and Morgan Stanley all had more than 100 subsidiaries in off shore tax havens. Citigroup has 90 subsidiaries in the Cayman Islands alone. JPMorgan Chase had 50 units, AIG and Wells Fargo each had 18 units in tax havens; all these financial institutions (and many others with subsidiaries in off shore tax havens) received government bailout money. The tax rate for Goldman Sachs in 2008 was 1%.

By contrast, the population of the Cayman Islands is about 50,000 – roughly the same as Elkhart, Indiana. Elkhart is home to about 10 bank branches. Elkhart has no known hedge funds. The Cayman Islands are home to 279 banks and 10,000 registered hedge funds. The other big difference is that the people of Elkhart pay their fair share of taxes while at least 83 of the top 100 corporations in America evade taxes by setting up dummy units in the Caymans. These large corporations siphon at least $100 billion tax dollars per year out of the US economy, and that's just through this one type of tax dodge. The lost tax money does not trickle back; it does not pay for hospitals, health care, schools, roads, fire stations, or our military.

Nobody likes to pay taxes but we can recognize the necessity; the alternative being anarchy. We have a tax system that is considered progressive. It is designed to tax the rich at a higher rate than the poor – at least that is the theory.

Adam Smith, considered the father of economic theory, explained the rationale for such a system: "The necessaries of life occasion the great expense of the poor. They find it difficult to get food, and the greater part of their little revenue is spent in getting it. The luxuries and vanities of life occasion the principal expense of the rich, and a magnificent house embellishes and sets off to the best advantage all the other luxuries and vanities which they possess. A tax upon house-rents, therefore, would in general fall heaviest upon the rich; and in this sort of inequality there would not, perhaps, be anything very unreasonable. It is not very unreasonable that the rich should contribute to the public expense, not only in proportion to their revenue, but something more than in that proportion."

President Theodore Roosevelt understood the fairness of a progressive tax, as outlined in his New Nationalism Speech: "No man should receive a dollar unless that dollar has been fairly earned. Every dollar received should represent a dollar's worth of service rendered, not gambling in stocks, but service rendered. The really big fortune, the swollen fortune, by the mere fact of its size, acquires qualities which differentiate it in kind as well as in degree from what is possessed by men of relatively small means. Therefore, I believe in a graduated income tax on big fortunes."

In that same speech, Roosevelt quoted President Abraham Lincoln in describing the nature of money: "Labor is prior to, and independent of, capital. Capital is only the fruit of labor, and could never have existed if labor had not first existed. Labor is the superior of capital, and deserves much the higher consideration." Both Lincoln and Roosevelt were referencing Aristotle and the Bible.

It is impossible to conceive of a fair tax system without considering the nature of money and usury. Money, in and of itself, does not produce anything of value. And usury allows someone to gain wealth without working for it. So we are faced with a choice to tax something that produces nothing of value, or to tax something that provides value.

Taxes are used to alter behavior. If we place a heavy tax on alcoholic beverages, fewer people drink as much. If we have a low tax on milk, people are likely to drink more milk. If we place a high tax on gasoline, people will drive less. When the burden of taxation is applied to labor, it deters production and value. If that burden is lessened, then production improves and value increases. When that burden is taken away from speculative capital, the speculation will become more reckless, but produce nothing of value.

There is a direct correlation between lower marginal tax rates on the upper end of income, and extreme economic volatility. Periods of low taxes on big fortunes result in a greater concentration of capital in the hands of a few individuals and corporations and greater speculation. The burden for maintaining the nation's infrastructure and global competitiveness falls on, and hampers productive labor. Speculation increases, and a single economic blow or a wrong bet can wipe out huge swaths of wealth in the blink of an eye. It was true in the 1920s and it is true today. Periods of high taxes on big fortunes have resulted in more stable economies and growth in productivity.

When a heavy tax burden is imposed on big fortunes the revenue is used to pay for the common property and resources that allowed the wealth to be accumulated. There is not a single wealthy American that has not benefitted from the combined greatness of America's infrastructure of roads, bridges, railways, airports, hospitals, schools; and from the natural resources of our forests, rivers, lakes, and oceans; and from the protections afforded by our police, firefighters, and courts; and from the freedoms fought and paid for by our military; and the goods and services produced by labor. The CEO of any major bank would not be so smug about their exorbitant salaries if there was no electricity, water, police protection, or trash collection.

But taxing income is equated with regulating pay. Some people work very hard, they train for years in their given profession, and they reasonably want to be paid more. Other people do not work so hard and are not proficient in their work, and it is reasonable they should be paid less. Fair enough, but that does not prove that inequality of work should be uncontrolled, it only argues that pay should be proportional to work; and that is not the case.

Take the example of John Thain, the infamous former CEO of Merrill Lynch who raked in $87 million in 2007. Despite the fact that Thain mismanaged the company to the edge of collapse, I have no doubt that he was a hard worker and probably worked many late nights and even weekends; for this he deserved to be paid more than someone who did not put in the same hours. He undoubtedly trained and studied for his career; for this he also deserved compensation. Thain also carried the responsibility of managing the risk of Merrill Lynch; for this, he also deserved compensation. But what is reasonable? Was Thain ultimately two or three times more productive than a co-worker? Was Thain 4,281 times more productive than a Private First Class? Impossible! If that was the case we could just round up 100 men with the work ethic of John Thain, send them to Iraq and Afghanistan and squash terrorism in a matter of days. When Thain failed to manage risk at Merrill Lynch he retreated to his mansion with hundreds of millions of dollars. If a soldier in Afghanistan fails to manage risk, he faces death for himself and his brothers in arms. It is beyond insanity to suggest that we have an economy that provides pay proportionate to work.

After years of deregulation and tax breaks for the wealthy, we see a situation where the second wealthiest man in America, Warren Buffett, paid a lower tax rate (17.7%) than his secretary (who paid 30% in federal taxes on an income of $60,000). Our current tax code is riddled with loopholes and complexity that make it ripe for abuse. Capital gains and some dividends are taxed at 5% to 15%, and capital gains are exempt from Social Security and Medicare taxes, but not labor income. Incomes above the cap ($97,500 for year 2009) are exempt from Social Security taxes. Even Buffett admits, "The tax system has tilted toward the rich in the past 10 years." More precisely, we have a regressive tax where the wealthy do not contribute proportionately to their income.

So, how can we control compensation in a way that eases the burden on production and increases the burden on disruptive speculation? There are two ways: progressive taxation, and limitations on usury.

Chapter 28

Usury is Regressive Taxation – Usury Hammers the Rest of Us

Usury modifies certain behavior, the same as taxation modifies behavior, but usury is regressive taxation. The burden of usury hits hardest on the poor, the working class, and the middle class but it imposes no burden on the wealthy. That's right – no burden on the wealthy, because the tax is passed on to the poor in the form of usury.

If someone purchases a bond that requires a tax on the interest collected, that bond pays a higher interest rate than a tax-free bond. A tax-free municipal bond may pay 4% while a taxable bond might pay 7%; the holder of the bond collects the same amount. The amount of interest is in direct proportion to the perceived risk, whether it's the risk of default or the risk of taxation. Taxable interest is always calculated and included in any loan. The bonded debt of a city, state, or nation is ultimately collected from productive labor. Likewise, a mortgage on property is collected from the tenant or the homebuyer;

they must pay the rent or mortgage with their productive labor; the landlord or lender just collects the rent. Usury transfers wealth from the producers and redistributes it to the wealthy.

Usury punishes production and encourages speculation. Note that I said "usury" punishes production, not that lending discourages production. A loan or capital investment is sometimes the only way to get a business started. The loan can pay for tools or equipment and the borrower uses the tools of her trade to start producing goods or services of value; when value is received, a portion is used to repay the loan. Usury is the premium or gain on the loan, and the borrower must consider this cost when acquiring a loan. Will she be able to produce enough value to repay both the principal and the interest, keeping in mind that the interest is compounding? It turns a challenge into a daunting challenge. When interest rates are low, it encourages business investment and productivity increases. When rates are high, it discourages business investment.

The Federal Reserve uses interest rates as a tool to slow the economy or speed up the economy. When the Fed raises rates, it dries up demand - sales drop, prices drop, more businesses fail, and there are even fewer jobs. The burden falls on the worker. This is usury as a regressive tax.

When the economy slows down, the Federal Reserve lowers interest rates and floods the economy with debt. When the Federal Reserve increases the nation's money supply to give a boost to the economy, they don't give the money directly to taxpayers, they give the money to the bankers, and the bankers put the money into circulation through loans – they flood the economy with debt. Usury causes debt to rise exponentially (due to the power of compounding). Workers can try to work harder. Productivity may grow by 3% or 4% but interest rates are usually much higher. Even when the Fed lowered rates to 1%, the public did not get that rate because the bankers tacked on their profits. It is impossible for productivity to keep pace with usury; not because the American worker is lazy, but because banks stopped lending capital for new factories and tools to equip workers to extend efficiencies as far as possible. And when American workers could not keep pace with usury, their jobs were shipped overseas.

Chapter 29

Money Seeks Money – Why Usury Shipped American Jobs Overseas

Money will seek the greatest returns. People who have money to invest have two basic options: invest in production or usury. When there were caps on usury, money found the greatest returns by investing in production. Investing in production carries risk; the business might fail or the business might be profitable. Honest capitalism is demanding. It requires constant innovation and a steady stream of new products. The horse and buggy are replaced by the car; the telegraph is replaced by the telephone; the abacus and the typewriter are replaced by the computer. Without innovation capitalism collapses, or at least begins a long process of deterioration. Direct investment in businesses, industry, and production requires effort.

Usury requires almost no work; a contract is written and the money is counted as the loan is repaid. If the borrower does not pay, the usurer can take whatever security was offered as collateral on the loan; borrowers are charged higher rates on unsecured loans and if the unsecured loan defaults, the usurer can send out debt collectors. In 1978, interest rate caps were basically eliminated and investors could get higher interest on loans, and the loans were not as difficult as investing in a business. It was a way to accumulate wealth without work. The economic landscape started to change.

Capital shifted into the financial sector and away from productive businesses. Two of the biggest businesses, General Motors and Sears, became examples of this shift; both increased their focus to their finance units. For a while, General Motors and Sears made more money on financing than profit on the actual sale of cars or appliances. Car making became secondary to finance, and when GM couldn't sell enough cars to keep the finance unit busy, they branched out into mortgages, revolving credit, and banking (GMAC and Ally).

There are two ways to increase production: invest in infrastructure, tools, equipment, and factories, and retain skilled workers to improve efficiencies - or cut costs. Capital was shifted to usurious finance and away from paying skilled workers and improving infrastructure. To keep costs low, production was sent offshore to countries that offered cheap labor and lax environmental standards. In order to conduct business with the US, countries were forced to hold capital reserves in dollars, or dollar denominated assets, such as US Treasury bonds.

The US dominance as a leader in manufacturing began to wane. Trade deficits increased and the deficits were financed with more debt in the form of Treasury notes and bonds, which put fresh capital into the money supply, and that fresh capital was soaked up by the financial sector. US manufacturing workers lost good paying jobs, yet at the same time they were encouraged to increase consumption; and they did; borrowing from the future to pay for the present. Cars, electronics, clothing, furniture, almost everything comes from overseas. Even American flags are now made in China. Don't blame the Chinese workers, or the Taiwanese, Korean, Honduran, or Bangladeshi workers. The loss of solid, skill based manufacturing jobs can be laid at the feet of the bankers. Money seeks the greatest return and the greatest returns came from high interest rates, not investment in business infrastructure. This is why jobs were shipped overseas; the root cause is usury – it's easier and it pays better.

The transformation of the US from a manufacturing giant to a consuming giant did not take place overnight. It took time for Americans to get buried under debt, it took time to for foreign governments to buy massive chunks of our debt, but the bankers were no longer constrained by caps on usury. When the bankers ran out of new debt to foist on the consuming public, they started funneling money into derivatives of debt. The bankers created an alphabet soup of strange and exotic instruments: CDO, CMO, MBS, CDS, and more. The derivatives market took the exponential growth of compound interest and added leverage. This was the usury equivalent of the Incredible Hulk on steroids. The derivatives market grew larger than the housing market, the stock market, the US economy, and the global economy – combined.

Leverage can be marvelous; bet $1 and get back $30. Leverage can also be hellish; bet $1 and lose $30. Banks can get rich fast by using leverage; they can also lose money fast by being leveraged. When the banks were making money fast, they did not save money for a rainy day, they did not set aside reserves to cover possible losses. The bankers wrote derivatives and called them reserves. And they sure as hell didn't invest in making America more productive. Americans are hard workers, but what made America a financial powerhouse was that Americans can work smart. Take away the investment in training and equipment and one American worker will not be more productive than 20 Chinese workers.

Why were American jobs shipped off to China? Because instead of investing in new factories, tools, and training, the bankers figured they could make more money speculating in casino markets –

trading derivatives, betting on leveraged buyouts, and speculating on Wall Street. It worked for a while, but all gamblers eventually lose.

Chapter 30

Fed Failure – Creating Money and Instability Out of Thin Air

Meanwhile, back on Main Street jobs were lost. Wages dropped. The average family had a negative savings rate and too much debt. By 2006, the general public had used up almost all of its collateral; charge cards were maxed out, houses were mortgaged to the hilt, and the federal deficit had ballooned. Supply exceeded demand. Wages could not support the debt service of the middle class. The economy contracted. The debt started to unravel. The response was entirely predictable - raise demand by increasing debt. The response was also entirely wrong; the problem was too much debt; the attempted solution was to increase debt even more. The Federal Reserve was trying to extinguish a fire by adding gasoline. The much better response would have been to cut the rate of usury to make debts service more reasonable.

The Federal Reserve's stated mission is to conduct the nation's monetary policy by influencing the monetary and credit conditions in the economy in pursuit of maximum employment, stable prices, and moderate long-term interest rates; to supervise and regulate banking institutions to ensure the safety and soundness of the nation's banking and financial system and to protect the credit rights of consumers; and to maintain the stability of the financial system and contain systemic risk that may arise in financial markets.

The Constitution states that Congress has the responsibility to conduct the nation's monetary policy, but the Federal Reserve has usurped that authority. Any honest review of the past 30 years would conclude that the Fed has failed its mission. The Fed's monetary manipulations led to the worst unemployment since the Great Depression, price volatility, excessive swings in interest rates (extremely low for member banks and excessively usurious for the general public), almost non-existent regulation of financial institutions, massive bank failures, and systemic risk that threatened to meltdown the global financial system. The Fed's manipulations did succeed in making the rich richer and the poor poorer.

The ever smaller and ever richer moneyed elite expanded its power. The Corporatists expanded their influence over governmental policy. The more subtle signs of the Corporatist coup were the multitude of legislative acts that favored the Corporatists and usurers over the citizens; the legal decisions that permitted criminal activity without criminal punishment (at most a rebuke or a slap on the wrist fine that could be written off as the cost of doing business); and the wholesale purchase of politicians and bureaucrats. The result of Corporatist Capitalism is ever increasing political instability. Americans are increasingly and intentionally divided, mainly over trivial issues. And as long as we remain distracted and divided, the less likely we are to confront the real culprits. The same Corporatists that championed free markets were more than willing to accept taxpayer bailouts. Privatize profits and socialize losses – and don't mess with the bankers' bonuses or they'll destroy your 401k. There has been no remorse from the bankers and that means they haven't learned a damn thing.

Where did the bailout money go? The Federal Reserve says they're not sure (although a good guess is that much of it is in off shore tax havens). How much bailout money did the Fed hand out to the banks? Again, the Fed says they don't have an accurate accounting. Has Congress audited the Federal Reserve to try and figure out where the money goes? Never. There are efforts in Congress, led by Rep. Ron Paul and Sen. Bernie Sanders (two of the most independent members of Congress), to force an audit. Paul and Sanders show their integrity and patriotism by challenging the bankers. Not surprisingly, the bill was largely gutted shortly after it was introduced. Federal Reserve Chairman Ben Bernanke is opposed to an audit: "I don't think it's (plan to audit the Fed) consistent with independence," Bernanke said of Paul's plan to subject the Fed to a Government Accountability Office (GAO) audit. "I don't think people want Congress making monetary policy."

Really, one day Bernanke needs to read the Constitution, specifically Article 1 Section 8, and particularly those lines that deal with Congressional authority "To borrow money on the credit of the United States" and "To coin money, regulate the Value thereof".

Which again raises the unanswered question: Why the hell do we need a middleman to print our own money?

Abraham Lincoln said: "Money is the creature of law, and the creation of the original issue of money should be maintained as the exclusive monopoly of the National Government. The privilege of creating and issuing money is not only the supreme prerogative of Government, it is the Government's greatest opportunity."

In 1964, Congressman Wright Patman said: "In the US today, we have in effect two governments. We have the duly constituted government, then we have an independent, uncontrolled and uncoordinated government in the Federal Reserve, operating the money powers which are reserved to Congress by the Constitution."

It's worse than Patman could have imagined. Now we have an elected government, hand-picked and financed by Corporatists and Plutonomists; and we have the Fed, a private oligarchy of 12 bankers which creates our money, regulates the amount in circulation, regulates the interest rate at which money shall be loaned to us, to businesses and to our government, whose sole legal obligation is to make as much profit for bankers as possible. How can a private institution regulate its shareholders? This tiny private bankers' oligarchy exercises control over our government, our economy, and our well being. The Fed can refuse to finance reforms and programs enacted by our constitutional government. The Fed can and does lobby Congress extensively, directly injecting itself into the political process.

Chapter 31

When Bubbles Pop – Quick Collapse, Slow Collapse, Demolition, and Devaluation

Inflation has overturned centuries of economic wisdom. In certain circumstances, credit can help increase productivity and boost economic growth, but there is a massive difference between borrowing to consume beyond one's means, and borrowing to increase one's means. Inflation has blurred that difference. In an inflationary environment there is (faulty) logic in borrowing as much as you can grab. What could be more advantageous than to buy an appreciating asset with depreciating currency? It seems like a quick and easy path to prosperity. Why work when you can consume, and get paid for it? Why invest in production when asset values inflate like helium balloons with no need for the sweat of production? Like most get rich quick schemes it is pure speculation. Price stability has been replaced by constantly rising prices but that doesn't make the increase stable. Balloons can be overinflated. Assets can be overinflated to the point of creating bubbles. The most likely outcome: Pop!

Inflation works like a tax. It taxes both the borrower and the lender. The tax burden is harder on the poor than the rich; it is a regressive tax. The burden hits the elderly trying to survive on savings from a lifetime of labor. The burden hits the worker whose productivity can't keep pace with the constant gains of speculation, inflation, and usury.

We have transformed from producers to consumers and the result is radical inequality. The US and Canada represent 5% of the world's population yet account for 32% of consumption. Western Europe represents 6.5% of the global population and 29% of consumer spending; and so, less than 12% of the world population controls almost 60% of the global consumer spending. Sub-Saharan Africa contains 12% of the world's population but only controls 1.25% of consumer spending. Usury fuelled capitalism does a terrible job of efficiently allocating resources. Usury forces over-consumption, and if there is not enough in the budget, then we are encouraged to borrow more; as individuals and as a nation we dig a deeper and deeper hole of debt.

The usury driven market must either grow or expire. There is not enough wealth in the world to pay for one penny of debt drawing compound interest over the past 2010 years. We can't produce and consume enough goods and services to keep up with the pace of usury. There are also limits on production. There is no natural growth that can match the exponential, infinite growth of compound interest. We can't grow infinite crops. We can't cut infinite timber, nor pump infinite oil. A borrowed dollar used to increase demand now, must decrease demand by that same dollar in the future, plus interest. This necessitates more borrowing.

When a family starts to accumulate debt, that debt will usually continue to build until they get rid of the debt through hard work, restraint, and discipline, or through bankruptcy. The budget of a nation works much like a household budget. People and governments almost always stay addicted to debt, until they are forced to quit.

The bankers have no intention of relinquishing their power. In recent history, our government feared the economy might collapse in 2001 and so Greenspan and Bush created more debt and the cash flowed, and the quick collapse was averted for a while. In 2008, the government feared the economy might collapse and so Bernanke and Bush, and later Obama, created more debt, and the cash flowed, and the collapse was averted for a while. The response was like trying to cure alcoholism by giving whiskey to a drunk; the shaking stopped, but the problem was really worse. You can't cure too much debt by issuing more debt.

Eventually the cost to service the debt, or pay the interest, becomes overwhelming. When economic growth doesn't keep up with debt and inflation created by usury, the result is: 1) quick economic collapse, 2) prolonged deflation, or devaluation of the currency to unwind the debt while trying to work through the systemic problems, 3) or a catastrophe (like war) to demolish the debt. Quick collapse, slow collapse, demolition; this has been the course of all economies throughout history.

The quick collapse is painful and shocking. In 1929, economists tried to hurry the collapse of the economy by following a policy of liquidation. Policy did not allow a choice between depression and no depression, but between depression now and a worse depression later. Any revival which is merely due to artificial stimulus leaves part of the work of depressions undone. Eventually, maladjustments in the economy have to be addressed, so the Hoover plan was to deal with the problems, and avoid a worse crisis down the road. President Hoover's economic team tried to purge the rottenness out of the financial system. This doctrine - that in the long run, the Great Depression would turn out to have been "good medicine" for the economy, involved liquidation – allowed major companies and significant industries to fail. The purge worked, but there was nothing left to stimulate. There was no new growth.

The slow motion version of economic collapse occurs when government debt becomes too large, or when paying the interest on the debt becomes too burdensome; the government will typically try to debase its own currency to try to repay the debt with cheaper dollars; it happened in 1933 and again in 1971. The slow collapse is painful. The economy continues to suffer. Spending power plunges and the cost of living soars. Bankruptcies skyrocket. Savings are wiped out. People suffer. The consumer debt economy will eventually stop muddling through. An exogenous event might cause the economy to crash, or it might linger. All the while the economy tries to repair itself. The real cause, the root cause, the malignant cancer - is usury.

Any recovery must eliminate excessive usury and turn that unproductive money to productive use. If we do not deal with usury, then we are just playing theoretical and ideological games that only provide artificial stimulation and will not avoid a collapse. It really doesn't matter whether we have a quick or a slow collapse, both are very painful. The real question is whether we purge the rottenness out of the system, and create a better way to move forward.

Chapter 32

Usury Enslaves – "But Our Slaves are Happy"

The consequences for the borrowers have been severe; they have lost more than they have gained. Look around you at friends and family who have lost jobs, homes, savings, dignity, and at the core they have lost their freedom. Some of the victims may have learned the age old truth that usury enslaves. Unfortunately, history has a habit of repeating.

"On the one side there is the party which holds the power because it holds the wealth; which has in its grasp all labor and all trade; which manipulates for its own benefit and its own purposes all the sources of supply, and which is powerfully represented in the councils of State itself. On the other side there is the needy and powerless multitude, sore and suffering. Rapacious usury, which, although more than once condemned by the Church, is nevertheless under a different form but with the same guilt, still practised by avaricious and grasping men… so that a small number of very rich men have been able to lay upon the masses of the poor a yoke little better than slavery itself." - Pope Leo XIII, in 1878.

Financial servitude was the basic idea behind slavery. One person purchased another person. After slavery was abolished in the US, financial servitude continued with the sharecroppers. The landowner rented out acreage to the sharecroppers, he bought their crops, and made the market in the crops, owned the house the sharecropper lived in, charged rent, and controlled the income of the sharecropper through the markets he controlled. Even when the sharecropper produced a big harvest, the excess supply pushed prices lower. The rent and interest always topped the increase in income. The poor sharecropper could not break free of the chains of usury.

No one prefers to be in debt. Debts are chosen as the least of the evils. The person who takes a mortgage knows they will not own the house until they have paid for two, three, or four houses over the full term of the loan, but the necessity of having shelter wins. The entrepreneur that takes a loan will work hours each day to repay the loan, and many hours more to repay the usury on the loan. The borrower truly becomes the servant of the lender.

The usurer has no personal interest in his slave. He has no care for his health or his life. He may live in a different state or country.

The borrower may be nothing more than a numbered account. If the borrower dies there is no loss. The property is returned to the usurer or the debt is passed to the borrower's heirs. If the borrower fails for any reason, the property must be returned to the lender, but the lender is under no obligation to return the time, energy, production, and value he has extracted from the borrower. The only consolation for the borrower is that the distress of poverty is less than the agony of enslaving debt.

The usurer claims that he is a real benefit to the borrower. The usurer may tout that they are the bank of opportunity, the source of opportunity for advancement that could not otherwise be found. No matter how well disguised by modern advertising, this is the same old claim of all those who appropriate the labors of their slaves. The slave owner could point to his well fed, well clothed, and happy slaves. The slave master could proclaim that his slaves were far better off and far happier than they could be in freedom. Their well kept condition and apparent happiness did not make them free. They were slaves, even if they accepted their condition without revolt. The usurer's victim is not free. Even if the borrower accepts debt to independence, that does not make him free.

Chapter 33

Equality of Opportunity – The Destruction of Special Privilege

Compound interest draws in wealth day after day, generation after generation and concentrates wealth in the hands of a few. A usurer in any community will absorb the wealth of that community in a relatively short time, even if the original loan amount is modest and even though the usurer does not produce any goods for the community. For every shirt sewn, every loaf of bread baked, every mile driven, every nail hammered, and every letter mailed, the usurer takes a cut. Wealth is redistributed from the borrowers to the usurers. A banker may be a stupid dolt and still collect great wealth as long as he doesn't interfere with the usurious principle. Wealth is redistributed from the worker to the usurers. The US economy has seen a shift in the past 30 years. The financial sector was formerly responsible for 12% to 17% of corporate profits. Recently the financial sector has raked in 41% of the profits. The increase in profits carries special privileges, interests, and opportunities. The financial sector has sought and received government protection unlike any protections afforded any other sector of the economy. Many of the same bankers who caused the economic meltdown are still at their desks, still receiving gargantuan bonuses. The banking lobby that bought the votes of legislators still buys legal protection without reproach.

There is no question that great corporate wealth influences not just legislation, but also elections. The Constitution guarantees protection of property, and we must make that promise good. But it does not give the right of suffrage to any corporation. Corporate expenditures for political purposes, and especially expenditures by corporations that have direct business with the government, have been one of the principal sources of political corruption. Politicians may raise their hand in a solemn vow that they will not be influenced by corporate bribery, but with the other hand they accept campaign contributions.

Corporations and wealthy families also receive judicial advantage, using their wealth to wage court battles that ordinary citizens could never afford. The result is that corporations frequently break the law without serious penalty. A secondary result is that corporations frequently reach settlements without admitting or denying guilt or innocence; fines are just the cost of doing business.

The 1960's saw the introduction of President Kennedy's Consumer Bill of Rights and a variety of popular laws such as truth in packaging and truth in lending. Several business lobbying organizations opposed the legislation and the establishment of a Consumer Protection Agency. The CPA was ultimately defeated in 1978. Apparently it is not a good thing to know what is really in a box of corn flakes or to be told the truth about a loan. Current attempts to protect consumers from abuses by the financial industry find the bankers sharpening their knives for battle and reviving their old rhetoric. At least some of the banking lobbyists' efforts will be paid by taxpayer bailout money. Heaven forbid the bankers are unable to continue writing predatory loans and hiding excessive fees.

In almost every struggle to improve the human condition, one of the main objectives has been to achieve equality of opportunity. One of the chief factors in progress is the destruction of special privilege. The essence of the struggle boils down to taking from some person, or class, or group of people the right to enjoy power, or wealth, or position, or immunity which has not been earned by service to their fellows. The conflict between people who possess more than they have earned and the people who have earned more than they possess is the key factor in progress. Our current struggle for progress pits ordinary citizens struggling for the right of self-government against special interests, who corrupt the workings of free government into machinery for defeating the popular will. The essence of the struggle is to equalize opportunity, destroy privilege, and afford the highest possible value to each individual life and to the country as a whole.

You never get perfect justice. Equality of opportunity means every man or woman will have a fair chance to make of himself all that he or she has the inherent capacity to achieve; the opportunity to reach the highest point that their capacities can carry them, unassisted by special privilege of their own, and unhampered by special privilege of others; the opportunity to get for himself and his family substantially what he or she has earned. Equality of opportunity also means the country and the community will get the highest service each citizen is capable of giving. Equality of opportunity means that everyone has a level playing field and fair play under the present rules of the game, and it also means changing the rules to work for more substantial equality of opportunity and more substantial reward for equally good service; it does not mean a lazy person is entitled to the same rewards as a hard worker.

The only way to create equality of opportunity and a level playing field is to remove the influence and control of special interests. Even though special interests are entitled to justice, they are not entitled to vote, they are not entitled to write legislation, they are not entitled to a voice on the bench. Wealth and property should be the servant, not the master of our country. It is essential to control the mighty commercial forces we have created. There can be no effective control of corporations when corporations control political activity. We must have transparency and publicity of corporate affairs to be certain corporations obey the law, and whether their management entitles them to the confidence of the public. We must have supervision of corporate capitalization, especially in the financial sector. If a bank is to be trusted with depositors' money they must prove they are deserving of that trust, not taking the money and gambling for quick profits. Officers and directors should be held personally responsible when any corporation breaks the law.

Corporations may offer shareholders protection from financial liabilities, but those protections are not a license to steal or kill.

Many people probably think equality of opportunity and the concepts laid out in the preceding three paragraphs are radical ideas; maybe it was when President Theodore Roosevelt presented these ideas in 1910 in his speech on a new nationalism; maybe it was radical when Abraham Lincoln signed the Emancipation Proclamation. Today, most reasonable people support the idea of equal opportunity for women, minorities, and everyone – make of it what you can. Yet the same obstacles that Roosevelt faced are still with us today. The playing field has not been leveled. The moneyed special interests are still corrupting politics. The mighty commercial forces still operate with impunity, and without effective controls and transparency.

We still have inequality. There is inequality among men and women, among young and old, and among black and white. These inequalities still cry for equality of opportunity and must be addressed. There is an even greater inequality right now; rich versus poor, specifically the wealthy usurers versus the middle and working class. Stopping the abuses of the bankers does not limit any individual's ability to work hard and be rewarded for their accomplishments. The greatest obstacle to progress for individuals and the nation as a whole is the enslaving chains of debt and usury. We're all in the same boat. The welfare of all of us is fundamentally dependent on the welfare of all of us, not on the usurious profits of a few of us.

Developing countries spent years repaying billions of dollars in loans, most of which had been accumulated under corrupt regimes. These debts undermined the ability of many countries to invest in their people and make progress fighting poverty, and many countries ended up spending more each year paying back old debts than they did on health and education combined. It really seemed insane that third world countries were forced to pay interest on debts while their citizens starved to death. A global movement demanded debt forgiveness. Wealthy countries and international financial institutions have taken action to cancel debts in many of the most impoverished countries, but there is still more to do to ensure these benefits are fully delivered, that other poor countries in need qualify, and that the countries that do benefit are not at risk of a future debt crisis. In total, nearly $110 billion worth of debt has been canceled since 1996, $93 billion of which was in sub-Saharan African countries. This relief has helped free up scarce resources for poor governments to invest in their people. Many African governments used their debt savings to eliminate primary school fees, which helped open school doors for millions of the poorest children. Other countries targeted their savings towards improving health services. Remarkably, many people have realized that cancelling the debt of third world countries increases the prosperity of those countries and allows them the opportunity to lift themselves out of poverty; less remarkable is that we haven't taken the lesson and applied it to debt in general.

Chapter 34
War – What if There Was a War and the Bankers Couldn't Profiteer?

In 1694 King William of Orange was preparing to go to war against France's King Louis XIV. King William could not get Parliament to fund his excursions (William was Dutch) and so he turned to William Patterson to print money through the creation of the Bank of England and central banking was born. The first job of central banking was to fund war. The Federal Reserve was created in 1913, and soon after the US entered World War I. Wars are expensive. Wars require expensive tools and those tools do not wear out over time, they get blown up and must be replaced in quick order. There is no doubt some wars are necessary and must be funded. There is also no doubt that some wars are not necessary and if they were not funded, they might be prevented. Gandhi once said, "Poverty is the worst form of violence." To which we can add "debt is the worst poverty". The corollary is that usury is the greatest deterrence to peace.

The history of the world shows that a condition of war results in the opportunity to foist debt upon free people. The bankers don't care about human suffering and shed blood, if riches can be increased. When concessions can be secured and people exploited for profit, the cry of suffering and the begging for mercy and the calls for justice are all in vain. Throughout history, the greedy bankers and their Corporatist politicians that are not required to shed their own blood have been willing to sacrifice the blood of others, if the price is right. Reporter Lesley Stahl on US sanctions against Iraq: "We have heard that a half million children have died. I mean, that's more children than died in Hiroshima. And, you know, is the price worth it?" Secretary of State Madeleine Albright: "I think this is a very hard choice, but the price--we think the price is worth it." The best possible way to stop war is to make it unprofitable.

When the politicians and the Corporatists are forced to deplete the Treasury and waste their own wealth instead of increasing it, they will stop the slaughter and peace will reign. Eliminate national debts and interest bearing bonds to pay for war and make the present wealth bear the present duty, and not slough off that duty on future generations. Test the patriotism of the usurers by making war a real sacrifice of their wealth, while they demand the ultimate sacrifice from our sons and daughters when their blood is poured on the field. War can never be an advantage to the usurer to increase his riches. When one of America's truest heroes gives their life for their country, we cannot allow profiteering to be more sacred than a hero's blood. Let the rich grow poorer with each day a war drags on. Let wealth be consumed rather than borrowed and compounded. Let the usurers face absolute poverty while our heroes face death on the field. While the greedy banker is permitted usury, he will use it, even if it means oppressing the world. When the gains of usury are utterly removed from war, and war consumes the wealth, even the greediest banker will beg for peace.

Chapter 35

Moral Hazard – Plausible Deniability: The Bankers Blame You

Moral hazard means that people with insurance may take greater risks than they would without insurance, because they know they are protected, so the insurer may get more claims than it bargained for. If you have car insurance, you might be less attentive to locking your car, because insurance would cover the cost of replacement. The term has been around for a long time and mainly used in connection with insurance and finance.

When the depression started with growing defaults on subprime loans, the bankers dusted off the idea of moral hazard. They refused to modify abusive and predatory mortgage loans on the theory that if they showed compassion and decency toward one unfortunate family then all their other victims would stop paying their mortgages and beg for relief. CNBC reporter Rick Santelli unleashed a torrent of criticism from his post at the commodity trading pits in Chicago. Santelli said: "Government is promoting bad behavior. . . . Do we really want to subsidize the losers' mortgages? This is America! How many of you people want to pay for your neighbor's mortgage?" The commodity traders cheered the Corporatist rant. Ironically, within months, taxpayers were forced to pay for the bankers' bad behavior.

The location, the commodity trading pits, was a bizarre place to ask the question but not nearly as bizarre as the question itself. The better questions would have been, "Do we really want our friends, neighbors, and family to suffer a predatory mortgage loan in order to pad the profits of the banks? And what are the consequences if we do nothing about the problem? Do we really want to lose $5 trillion in wealth rather than show compassion?"

Predatory loans almost inevitably lead to default. The terms are so abusive that most people can't hope to make payments. The banks knew the terms. The banks wrote the terms. They securitized the loans and sold them fast. The first wave of predatory loans to default were subprime mortgages, followed by Option ARMs, followed by Alt-A loans, followed by jumbo loans, followed by prime mortgage loans. Not all these types of loans were predatory but the predatory loans kicked off a chain reaction of defaults, which resulted in foreclosures, which pushed down home prices, which resulted in negative equity, which resulted in more defaults, which resulted in more foreclosures, which resulted in even lower home prices. That, in turn, caused mortgage based derivatives to default, which kicked off a death spiral of other derivatives, which wiped out several banks and insurance companies. The bankers looted the Treasury, with the complicity of the government; everything continued to spiral down.

If the original predatory mortgages had not been based on excessive usury, they never would have defaulted, or the defaults would have been manageable. People could have stayed in their homes and the housing market would have enjoyed much more stability. Once upon a time (pre-1978), there were caps on usury. Loans were not typically abusive, except for illegal loan sharks. Once upon a time borrowers felt a strong moral obligation to repay their debt. Once upon a time, there was a sharp stigma attached to default. We have all heard stories about the small town grocer or hardware store which extended credit when a customer was down on their luck and eventually the borrower made good, if it was possible. You've probably seen the movie *It's a Wonderful Live* which airs relentlessly around Christmas. Jimmy Stewart played the small town owner of a Savings and Loan; he made fair and honest loans, and when he got in trouble, the customers volunteered to bail out the S&L. If Stewart's character had charged excessive usury and foreclosed on homeowners, he might have suffered a different fate.

The Supreme Court has determined that corporations have a type of "personhood" but it is an illusion; corporations have economic and physical qualities but they still lack the ethical and moral responsibility of personality. Corporations employ real people but that does not give a corporation personhood. Personality must always be considered or there are no rights to be considered. Property must always have an owner. Labor can't happen without a laborer. Otherwise there are only physical forces and material things; the sun shines and a tree grows; the winds blow and the tree topples. Incorporation allows owners to be insulated from the liabilities and responsibilities of the work done on behalf of the corporation. The owners can hire managers and workers, and if their labor does not earn a satisfactory dividend for the owner, the employees are discharged. If a product results in death or injury, the corporate ownership faces no personal liability. Incorporated wealth cannot claim personal rights and yet escape personal responsibility, without creating a moral hazard; that would only encourage reckless corporate behavior. We have all experienced reckless corporate behavior and it is shrugged off with the explanation that it's not personal, it's just business.

You probably don't know the person who approved your mortgage loan. You don't know the person who approved your revolving loan for a credit card. You certainly don't know the fool who sent your dog a pre-approved credit card application. You probably don't know who to talk to if you face a problem and need leniency to allow you to "make good" on a loan. When the Federal Reserve cut interest rates beginning in 2001, the credit card companies did not pass the savings to you. The Fed rate dropped to one percent, but you're credit card rate just went higher. In 2002, credit card companies reaped a $10 billion windfall from lower rates and the savings were taken from you, not passed along to you. For the past 30 years (at least), corporations have displayed a distinct lack of personal responsibility.

There is little question that borrowers have changed. Americans have become addicted to debt, but Americans are still incredibly hard working and productive. What really changed? Usury has resulted in radical economic and societal shifts. The Corporatists have denied their accountability and demand that the rest of us pay for their mistakes. And still, most American want to "make good" on their debts, but at some point they have to do the math, and if the numbers don't work out, then any competent financial advisor would have to tell the family it is in their best interest to default. It's not personal, it's business.

And that is the lesson we have learned from the bankers: it's just business. And this is the real moral hazard the bankers now face. Ironically, it is known as the Golden Rule; do unto others as you would have them do unto you. What could be easier to understand? You know how you would like to be treated – that's how you should treat others. Maybe it is just "business" but that is not an excuse for abusive, dishonest, impersonal behavior. Some people might consider stealing cars to be their business, but the majority has outlawed car theft. We also have laws that say our medicines can't be tainted, our appliances must not be built to explode in our face, our cars must meet certain safety standards, our food must be handled in a sanitary manner, a pound must weigh a pound, a gallon must measure a gallon, and in a time of extreme emergency (hurricanes, earthquakes, wildfires) a retailer can't gouge prices and charge $100 for a bottle of water.

The free market is a myth. We do not have free markets and we do not want free markets. We need some rules to follow. We want and need referees to keep the game fair. We don't allow a football game to be played with guns and knives. Disclosures are not meant to hide deceit behind fine print. Contracts do not create a license to steal. We want honest, fair markets where people interact with integrity and decency, and as long as the game is played square, we don't want the referees to get in the way.

Capitalism is a great economic system only when there is honesty, fairness, equality of opportunity, and reasonable rules are followed. We do not have that in America at this time. Capitalism has failed. We can either fix what is wrong with capitalism or we will end up with a different economic system. No instrument of oppression ever surpassed in severity the usury of incorporated wealth and still managed to maintain the illusion of respectability. We need to reconsider the laws that prevent bankers from stealing.

We need to think about the rules that must be observed to create equality of opportunity. We need to reconsider how to channel capital to its highest and best use. Capital is a finite asset. If it is used for one place it cannot be used for another. If the capital is not employed in an industry that makes efficient use of it then we are misusing our capital resources. Do we want the capital of America tied up in usurious schemes? It makes no sense to allow the bankers to suck money out of the economy, to get wealth without work. The economy serves the bankers, rather than the other way around. The tail wags the dog. We have some choices to make. The simple truth is you can spend your money better than the bankers can spend your money.

Section Five – How to Serve Bankers: A Recipe with 12 Steps

Chapter 36
The Debate – Debunking Myths

With any luck you now understand that usury is bad. Usury centralizes wealth in the hands of the unproductive few. Usury is a regressive tax that has created an unprecedented disparity between rich and poor, not just in the US but also globally. Usury creates inflation and destabilizes the economy. Usury is the root cause behind the loss of solid middle class jobs that have been shipped offshore. Usury shifts investment capital away from production and into the unproductive financial sector, creating a speculative and risky casino mentality towards investing. Usury promotes a culture of greed. Usury plunders nations and facilitates war. Usury extracts a pound of flesh from everyone, even if you as an individual try to avoid debt. And if you get caught in the trap of debt, usury enslaves. This is what we learn if we listen to the distilled wisdom of all the generations that came before us: Abraham Lincoln, Andrew Jackson, Benjamin Franklin, Aristotle, Cato, David, Solomon, Buddha, Confucius, Mohammed, and Jesus. And for most of history, the greatest minds have considered usury to be pure evil.

It took a long time for people to be brainwashed into accepting usury as the norm. The rich get richer and the poor get poorer. This is not theory, it is historic fact; we tend to accept it as fact and think there is nothing we can do. Of course, the simple solution is to eliminate usury. The complete elimination of usury would put a stake through the heart of the blood sucking bankers, but let's be realistic – that's not going to happen. If we could start by re-instituting the legal caps on usury we would see huge improvements, but it won't be easy.

There will be people who argue for usury. They will claim that any cap on interest rates will dry up credit, especially for the poor. Financial institutions have always figured out how to conduct profitable business serving the middle class, and they will continue to do so under reasonable limits that protect the consumer. Credit can, and should be available, based upon a person's ability to repay the debt. It makes no sense to give someone a high interest credit card or an artificially inflated mortgage that resets to extremely high rates. The bankers are not lending to poor people to help them, they are lending to make the maximum profit. If the bankers really want to help poor people, they could make credit available and then reinvest their profits in projects that help lift people out of indebtedness - that's not happening.

The bankers will argue that if rates are capped then poor people will borrow excessively. The truth is that bankers have encouraged excessive borrowing among the worst credit risks, so long as they can charge high fees and high interest rates. Bankers have to learn to lend responsibly. Deploying capital to productive use creates opportunity and jobs.

Corporatist lackeys will argue that capping interest rates will result in higher costs for people with good credit. The banks have made excessive usury part of their business model. They are the modern day loan sharks, and they will issue threats just like any loan shark. Cutting rates does not result in higher costs – cutting rates lowers costs. Over time, banks will learn they can still make money with caps on usury. There is plenty of money in responsible lending to credit worthy customers, always has been. There is not enough money in responsible banking practices for wild, reckless gambling in unregulated derivatives.

The bankers will also argue that any restrictions on the financial sector will stifle innovation and slow our economic recovery. Hogwash! Financial innovation is a banking term that has become synonymous with screwing the customer, and gambling by the banks. Following the near collapse and bailout, lending dried up. The greatest impediment to honest lending is financial innovation. America created a strong and vibrant economy with reasonable caps on interest rates. We created jobs and had a healthy middle class. The re-institution of limits on usury will help put us on the road to recovery, and that economic recovery will not come by expanding the financial sector's casino.

Finally, the bankers will argue that any restrictions will just create an underground economy of completely unregulated loan sharks. The banks have been acting like unregulated loan sharks. Re-regulation would mean that anyone who charges excessive interest would be engaged in illegal loan sharking, and that should rightly carry criminal penalties. An underground economy probably will emerge, and it will probably consist of religious and social groups whose members contribute to help one another through difficult times. Americans are good about helping one another, or at least we once were.

It is all just wishful, pie in the sky thinking that the banks will argue a little, and then roll over and accept caps on usury. The merest hint of caps on usury will probably lead to big declines on Wall Street. This is simple truth; the bankers will throw a tantrum, like a spoiled kid; they won't care if they damage the economy or the nation as a whole. They will try to scare the wits out of us all. We've seen it before; in November 1991 the country was dealing with recession. President George H. W. Bush (the senior) was talking about his economic stimulus policies at a fundraiser in New York. President Bush included a simple, almost throw away mention in the speech, "I'd frankly like to see credit card rates down. I believe that would help stimulate the consumer and get consumer confidence moving again." Of course, the President was right.

The next day Senator Alfonse D'Amato of New York proposed national legislation to cap credit card interest rates at 14%. The legislation passed the Senate on a 74-19 vote the same day. The bankers panicked; they sent out the lap dog economists to proclaim that interest rate caps would result in massive bank failures; the stock market plunged. Vice President Dan Quayle announced that the President would veto any cap on credit card interest rates. The bankers had squashed any chance of reform. And if any new reform is now suggested you can bet the bankers will revert to their old playbook to squash reform again.

So how can we cap usury? How can we break the addiction to debt and usury? We need a 12 Step Plan. Any solution must be comprehensive; it must include re-regulation of the financial sector, campaign finance reform, Trust Busting to break up banks that are Too big to fail, an end to offshore tax havens, new regulations on credit rating bureaus, changes in bankruptcy laws, education to teach Americans how to get out of debt, and even a little civil disobedience. But the truth is that to get any of that accomplished we have to slip it past the bankers in such a way that they can't put up a fight.

So, here is the 12 Step Plan:

Chapter 37
Solutions:
STEP #1 – The Military Bank – The Best Deal: If it is Good Enough for Bankers, it is Good Enough for our Heroes

We start by creating a Military Bank.

The Military Bank can be created by an act of Congress to meet the legitimate credit needs of all active military personnel, including: Army, Navy, Air Force, Marines, Coast Guard, and Reserves. Any person who is good enough to stand in harm's way and shed blood for their country is good enough to be given a good deal. All active military personnel would be entitled to the best possible terms on legitimate credit that our country has to offer. In 2009, the Federal Reserve has been lending money to banks at a rate of approximately one-quarter of one percent to one-half of one percent (0.25% to 0.5%), therefore the Military Bank would offer loans to active military personnel at a rate not to exceed 0.25%. If the lowest interest rate (the Fed funds target rate) increases from its current historic low levels, then the interest rate offered to military could also increase, but be capped at a maximum of 5%. If it's good enough for the bankers it is good enough for America's greatest heroes that defend our freedom.

This does not mean that a Private First Class earning an annual salary of $20,322 per year would be entitled to borrow a billion dollars from the Military Bank. All lending would be based on legitimate need and legitimate ability to repay the debt. The Department of Defense could make financial advisors available to all personnel (they do that already) to offer guidance on the prudent use of credit. The Veterans Administration is in place and capable to help. Financial advisors could create a financial roadmap for all personnel and help establish uniform, consistent standards and amounts of available credit. The Military Bank would be available to all military that wishes to do business with the Bank; no personnel would be forced to do business with the Bank.

Article 1, Section 8 of the United States Constitution spells out the Powers of Congress and those powers include: "To make Rules for the Government and Regulation of the land and naval Forces; To provide for calling forth the Militia to execute the Laws of the Union, suppress Insurrections and repel Invasions; To provide for organizing, arming, and disciplining the Militia, and for governing such Part of them as may be employed in the Service of the United States" Further, the Constitution says Congress shall have the power to: "borrow money on the credit of the United States;" also, "To coin Money, regulate the Value thereof," and also, "to pay the Debts and provide for the common Defence and general Welfare of the United States". It seems pretty clear that Congress has the legal power to serve the banking and credit needs of the military. Why the hell should bankers be permitted to act as middlemen between our troops and the government that pays them? There is a long history, from colonial times to the Civil War, of our nation making direct payment to our soldiers.

The GI Bill was created in 1944 and it was one of the most significant pieces of legislation in American history. The GI Bill helped soldiers returning from war with cash payments while they were looking for work, money for education, and low interest, low down payment home loans. The GI Bill is probably the greatest single source of wealth creation ever. Eight out of ten men born in the 1920's were assisted by the GI Bill. Millions of GI's were able to further their education, start businesses, buy homes, and find jobs. By 1955, the country had gained 400,000 engineers, 200,000 teachers, 90,000 scientists, and 22,000 dentists. The GI Bill created a vast middle class following World War II, or at least it provided the equality of opportunity for millions of GI's to create a middle class. The GI Bill unleashed prosperity never before known, despite failing to accommodate many African American vets. Some people think the GI Bill is a huge welfare program. That is a lie. Every penny paid out to veterans was earned. There would not be one penny to pay out unless the veterans had done their jobs.

The GI Bill has been rewritten and updated several times since 1944, the "New GI Bill" of 2008 offers critical educational assistance to this generation's veterans. The bill fully covers college tuition up to the cost of the most expensive in-state public school, and a monthly living stipend is available. Both President Bush and Senator John McCain vehemently opposed it, claiming that it would decrease re-enlistment. Its cost for ten years is equivalent to just about one week of the Iraq war effort overall. Education for veterans is a sound investment in the future, and the least we owe the men and women who volunteered to serve our country.

All the various versions of the GI Bill have been noble, but not enough to keep pace with the inflationary demands of usury. By 2007, the median nationwide price of a home was $219,000, but the VA home loans only went up to $144,000. In 2006, at the peak of US subprime lending, the number of VA loans fell to barely a third the level of two years earlier, according to VA data. Troops turned to banks when our government was too stingy to meet their credit requirements, and the bankers spit in the faces of America's bravest. No one asked them for their credit score when we asked them to fight for us, but when active troops needed a place to live, the banks considered our troops to be a credit risk. Sure, the banks made home loans, but they frequently labelled the troops as subprime borrowers and slammed the troops with hidden fees and adjustable rates that jumped to excessive rates. There has never been and will never be anything "subprime" about an American soldier. It is bizarre to think that a soldier who might have his hand on an atomic bomb and is the guardian of our national security is nothing but a "credit risk" to the bankers; a soldier that can command a jet worth hundreds of millions of dollars is too risky for the bankers to extend a fair deal on a mortgage to house his family.

For far too long, the banks have treated the brave heroes of the military with the utmost contempt and hatred. Ground zero for foreclosures has been centered on military bases. Military personnel were targeted for subprime loans and when the egregious terms of those loans became evident, many soldiers' families faced eviction. That's just wrong. Our soldiers are poorly paid, so poorly paid that it is sometimes difficult to make the money stretch from paycheck to paycheck. Many soldiers were forced to resort to payday loans just to get by. The problem was so pervasive that legislation was finally written to limit payday loans to all military to a maximum of 36% annual percentage rate. Banks can make loans from the government for 0.25% and then turn around and lend the money to soldiers at 36%. That's just wrong. The lawmakers that wrote that legislation may have thought they were helping, after all 36% is a better rate than 420%, but the truth is they were still stabbing our soldiers in the back. Those lawmakers were too weak to demand a good deal for our troops. It's time to grow a spine.

Our troops deserve better pay. There is no justification for paying corporate mercenaries 8 times the pay of enlisted troops. Next, the GI Bill needs to be updated to meet the credit requirements of the troops. We need to give the troops the opportunity to break free of bankers that have abused troops in the past. The bankers have proven, through their deeds and actions, that they disrespect the uniform. The bankers have proven that they serve money above all else; they do not deserve the privilege of serving the banking and credit needs of America's heroes. A new GI Bill that includes a Military Bank could eliminate the need for a middleman that sucks out value from a soldier's hard earned pay. We could establish branches in every commissary of every military base and also offer secure on-line banking without hidden fees and without excessive usury. We just don't need the bankers for this job. The military will be better served by military personnel at the Military Bank.

If you oppose either or both of the current wars, that is your choice, and you are free to express your opinions. Remember that it is the politicians that push us into wars and it is the soldiers that deliver us into peace. I think most Americans would agree that our troops have earned our most complete respect. America's best deserve the best loan rates; they deserve better loan rates than we offer the bankers. The proposal for updating the GI Bill to include a Military Bank boils down to one question: Do you support our troops? You can either side with the troops or you can side with the bankers; if you do not stand with the troops you stand against them. And if you stand against the troops you'll have plenty of bad company: Hitler, Ho Chi Minh, Saddam Hussein, Osama bin Laden, Nazis, fascists, communists, terrorists, and the bankers.

And any person who is good enough to shed blood for their country is good enough to be given a good deal, now and in the future.

A new, revised GI Bill should include a Military Bank plus a Veterans Bank. Veterans have earned a good deal.

Next, we should make sure that the heroes in our own backyard are remembered. Police and Fire Fighters put their lives on the line every day. How about a Police Bank and a Fire Fighters' Bank?

And we have a long list of professions that get their pay checks directly from the government: teachers, jailers, scientists, clerks, forest rangers, border patrol agents, sanitation workers, health care professionals, FBI, CIA, Homeland Security, and more. Why should the banks siphon off huge chunks of each pay check?

But let's take this one step at a time. If we start with a Military Bank and a Veterans Bank it will let people see banking without excessive usury; it will show that we don't need bankers for all of our credit and banking needs. The non-usurious Military and Veterans Banks will prove to be a powerful economic stimulus. Money diverted from usury will circulate in the economy and be put to productive use. It will allow us to wean off our dependence on banks that have become so powerful they are too big to fail, and threaten our national security with the very real possibility of systemic financial collapse. The time has come to introduce true financial innovation. We currently have more than 8,000 banks and they are all serial usurers. Honest innovation would involve the introduction of non-usurious, low cost, customer oriented banking and credit. Could the commercial banks still compete? Sure, but they might have to give up their multi-million dollar bonuses and their gold plated toilets.

Can we really create a Military Bank? Will it work? Absolutely, the GI Bill proves it. Also, we have taken a step in this direction with student loans. In September 2009, legislation was passed that will drive banks out of the student loan business, instead relying on an existing government program to provide college financing. The bill's sponsor, Rep. George Miller of California said, "We can either keep sending these subsidies to banks, or we can start sending them directly to students." The bill blocks a planned bank increase in interest rates on student loans. The bill is expected to save $87 billion dollars in the next 10 years.

Chapter 38

STEP #2 – Campaign Finance Reform – Stop Bribery

Faced with the largest financial crisis since the Great Depression, and the largest transfer of wealth from the American people to the biggest banks in this country, you might think that every committee of Congress would be involved in hearings. You would be wrong. We have seen a few hearings on very arcane aspects of financial reform. We're going to have a consumer protection agency to help the poor consumer, who doesn't understand all of this, rather than hearings on the fundamental new architecture of reforming the American financial system. The Federal Reserve will be given more regulatory authority, even though they have shown no ability to regulate.

How serious is the government? Has the Justice Department hired new prosecutors? Has the FBI hired new agents? Has there been any prosecution of high level bankers? Bankers lost trillions of dollars, but committed no crimes? Bankers have hundreds of off-shore subsidiaries, but they're not evading taxes? The FDIC has identified more than 500 problem banks, but at their current pace, they get around to about 125 to 150 of those problem banks each year. Three of the five largest investment banks failed; the largest S&L failed; the fourth largest bank failed; hundreds of smaller banks have failed; the largest mortgage lender failed; the largest insurance company failed; Fannie Mae and Freddie Mac failed; private hedge funds failed; there were massive violations of lending laws; executives walked away with billions stuffed in their pockets; trillions of dollars were lost – and nobody broke the law. Justice? There are different rules for the Corporatists.

The single best investment — in terms of greatest return on invested dollars — has been the lobbying efforts of the major banks and finance firms. These firms' political activities have yielded them trillions of dollars in assorted bailouts, plus "get out of jail free" cards.

For 100 years after the Constitution was ratified, various governmental entities regulated corporations, cancelling their charters promptly if they compromised the public good in any way. The Supreme Court decided in 1886, in a case called *Santa Clara County v. the Southern Pacific Railroad*, that corporations were indeed legal persons, at least that is the accepted, though probably incorrect understanding. Since 1886, the public good was increasingly compromised—until it was finally displaced altogether.

In 2010, the Supreme Court removed the ban on political spending by corporations in candidate elections. The case, *Citizens United v. Federal Election Commission*, evolved from a documentary, "Hillary: The Movie", produced by the conservative nonprofit corporation Citizens United. Corporations and unions had been barred from spending their own treasury funds on advertisements that urge the election or defeat of a federal candidate. This restriction dates back to 1907, when President Theodore Roosevelt called on Congress to forbid corporations, railroads and national banks from using their money in federal election campaigns. The SCOTUS decision heralds a return to the bad old days of the robber barons. The Campaign Reform Act of 2002, also known as McCain-Feingold banned the broadcast, cable or satellite transmission of "electioneering communications" paid for by corporations in the 30 days before a presidential primary and in the 60 days before the general election. The ban applied to communications "susceptible to no reasonable interpretation other than as an appeal to vote for or against a specific candidate."

Two significant prohibitions on corporations were left standing. Corporations, and presumably unions, cannot give money directly to the campaigns of federal candidates (accounting details). The court also affirmed current federal rules which require the sponsors of political ads to disclose who paid for them, so at least we can see the enemy.

The lower court ruling which upheld current law was overturned on a 5-4 partisan decision.

Justice Anthony Kennedy wrote for the majority, "If the First Amendment has any force it prohibits Congress from fining or jailing citizens, or associations of citizens, for simply engaging in political speech."

What Kennedy delineated but could not distinguish is that there is a difference between citizens and associations of citizens. Citizens have the right to vote, one person one vote; associations of citizens (which might include non-citizens and multi-national corporations) do not have the right to vote. Make no mistake, corporations are not people and money is not speech. People are not property (the Civil War made that point) and property can never be human. What Kennedy really did was to smother the voice of citizens and destroy the power of the ballot.

Justice John Paul Stevens called the decision "a radical change in the law ... that dramatically enhances the role of corporations and unions -- and the narrow interests they represent -- in determining who will hold public office." Justice Stevens understates.

The Corporatists are now the ruling party. This change is more than radical, it is seismic and it is a shot to the heart of democracy. The coup has been bloodless but not without misery. Ordinary citizens struggled against special interest for the right of self-government; their progress measured by the destruction of special privilege. Blood has been spilled for the right of self-government. The essence of the struggle is to equalize opportunity, destroy privilege, and afford the highest possible value to each individual life and to the country as a whole. Democracy has never been won with bribes or mercenaries. The ideal is too precious for a cash price. It is a fool's fantasy to imagine you can amass a nest egg that will leave you unbothered by oppression. The Corporatist treason seems bland, but the grey flannel only masks a ruthless, savage, and all encompassing determination to rule. Freedom dies when rights and justice are determined by dollars.

Significant campaign finance reform is the greatest fear of the Corporatist Plutonomy. Every citizen only has one vote. The Plutonomists are outnumbered 99 to 1. Corporations and the wealthy elite try to influence your vote by financing campaigns and lobbying politicians. The Corporatists' most powerful tool is fear. They will try to convince you that they must be allowed to steal trillions of dollars in bailout funds or your IRA will collapse. They try to convince you that elders will be euthanized to provide health care for all. They try to convince you that immigrants are stealing your job so you won't notice that they have shipped all the good manufacturing jobs offshore. They threaten higher interest rates when confronted with the possibility of an audit. They try to convince you that the economy will collapse if they are forced to exercise common sense and prudence. As long as Corporatist money is allowed in politics fear mongering will prosper.

There are no easy answers for campaign finance reform. The current system is too corrupt for easy answers. How can you tell if a politician is corrupt? If they accept money from corporate interests – they are corrupt. If that sounds harsh, so be it. We elect people to represent We the People, that is how the Constitution was written.

There is a truth that has stood the test of time. It was true 2,000 years ago and it will be true in 2,000 years. "No one can serve two masters."

Chapter 39

STEP #3 – New Rules – You Can't Win a Rigged Game

The following exchange between Alan Greenspan, former Chairman of the Federal Reserve and Congressman Henry A. Waxman, Chair of the House Committee on Oversight and Government Reform, occurred at a hearing of that committee on October 23, 2008.

Chairman Waxman: "[In your statement, you said] "I do have an ideology. My judgment is that free, competitive markets are by far the unrivaled way to organize economies. We have tried regulation, none meaningfully worked." That was your quote. You have the authority to prevent irresponsible lending practices that led to the subprime mortgage crisis. You were advised to do so by many others. Now, our whole economy is paying its price. You feel that your ideology pushed you to make decisions that you wish you had not made?"

Mr. Greenspan: "Well, remember… ideology is a conceptual framework with the way people deal with reality. Everyone has one. You have to. To exist, you need an ideology. The question is whether it is accurate or not. What I am saying to you is, yes, I found a flaw…

in the model that I perceived is the critical functioning structure that defines how the world works, so to speak."

Chairman Waxman: "In other words, you found that your view of the world, your ideology, was not right, it was not working."

Mr. Greenspan: "Precisely. That's precisely the reason I was shocked."

Alan Greenspan is shocked. Just like the movie Casablanca, with Greenspan in the role of Captain Renault as he gathers his winnings from the casino: "I'm shocked, shocked to find that gambling is going on in here!" Nobody likes government to intrude on our work or our private life, and the best way to insure that government leaves you alone is to not intrude on others; the Golden Rule. If the bankers had conducted business in an honest, fair, reasonable, transparent, and legal manner then we would not need to regulate them. We would all say, "Leave those nice bankers alone and let them continue to do good work."

The flaw was not in the basic precept of capitalism; the flaw was the mistaken belief that capitalism could not be corrupted by unfettered greed. Deregulation has failed. The bankers, left to their own devices, screwed up the economy while stuffing cash into their own pockets; they had their chance at deregulation and they abused it. Meanwhile, people are kicked out of their homes, lose their retirement savings, lose jobs, and lose their voice in government. Yeah, everybody is shocked. The bankers must be regulated; further deregulation or lack of effective reregulation would certainly result in a complete systemic financial meltdown.

Here are a few key elements to effective regulation:

Repeal the Depository Institutions Deregulation and Monetary Control Act (DIDMCA) of 1980 which gutted the state laws that capped usury. No one should be exempt from usury limits. This radical experiment that legalizes loan sharks has proven to be a failure.

Reinstate the Glass-Steagall Act which built a wall between traditional banks and investment banks. Banks should be a safe warehouse for storing your savings. Banks should then take those deposits and make responsible loans within the community. Separating banks from brokerage firms guarantees that when Wall Street stumbles, it doesn't cause the banks to fall. Right now, banks are taking money and gambling. Goldman Sachs was an investment bank, a securities firm. When the crisis hit, Goldman changed to a commercial bank holding company; this allowed Goldman to have access to the Federal Reserve and tap into the nation's money supply. In the summer of 2009, Goldman became a financial holding company; this meant Goldman could borrow money from the Federal Reserve at almost zero percent, and then they could speculate however they want – they could buy stocks, bonds, businesses, derivatives, or they could just take the money to Las Vegas and put it on the craps table. And if it goes well, Goldman gets to keep the profits. If they lose their bets, the taxpayers are forced to pay. If you don't want to support Goldman's gambling habit, then we need to reinstate Glass-Steagall. If you want a safe place to store your savings, then we need to reinstate Glass-Steagall.

Repeal the Commodity Futures Modernization Act. This rule exempted derivatives from all the rules that affect every other financial instrument. This is a marketplace 45 times larger than the gross domestic product of the US with almost no regulation at all. The CFMA created a Wild West bonanza in the derivatives markets. If the quants could dream up a scheme, they would sell it, even if nobody understood it. Credit default swaps are sold to people who have no insurable interest, and they are sold without setting aside reserves to pay claims. This was the Mother of All Moral Hazards. Derivatives must be regulated and derivatives must have reserves to support their positions. Bankers should not be allowed to write a derivative to act as the cash reserve of another derivative – that is nothing but a Ponzi Scheme. Unregulated derivatives do not control risk, they create even bigger risk.

Overturn the Bear Stearns rule. The SEC's 2004 rule change eliminated the 12 to 1 leverage restrictions on banks in favor of capital requirements by type of asset – the result was leverage ratios that climbed to 33 to 1, and beyond. This allowed the bankers to place bigger and bigger bets, and encouraged a casino mentality. By allowing this incredible leverage, we have gotten away from the idea of a bank that accepts deposits from customers and then makes loans based upon deposits held. Eventually every gambler loses, and when they lose we are faced with forced deleveraging, bailouts, and a liquidity crisis.

Bonuses and compensation should be based on merit. High risk trades are risky to the economy, but not to the traders. Corporate liability creates a heads we win, tails you lose scenario for traders and their banks. By the time we are all asked to pay for their mistakes, they have collected their bonuses and face no more liability. Catastrophic losses are meaningless to the bankers once they clear the liability limits. There are now small steps being taken to limit executive compensation to bankers. This makes sense. Capitalism is based on risk and return, not risk and run away with the loot.

Regulate sub-prime lenders, mandate and enforce lending standards. This one is pretty self-explanatory; predatory lending was a key reason for the subprime debacle.

The best lending standard is based on a cap on usury.

Require mark to market accounting and require transparency in accounting. Some assets do not trade on a daily, or even a regular basis; what prices will you use for those? The answer now is to prepare the financial statements based on assumptions. In other words, make up a number. The opponents of mark to market claim that accurate accounting forces banks to write off loses before they are realized; forcing banks to raise capital to cover losses that may not materialize. They claim that given time, the losses might turn profitable – or not. The correct answer is not to make up numbers, but to set aside adequate reserves to cover losses. If today's losses turn to profits in the future, then the reserves can be adjusted accordingly. Accounting has become an exercise in obfuscation. The loss of faith in accounting's ability to provide full disclosure in financial statements is an attack on one of the core elements of investment decision making, and off-balance sheet items are major culprits. Accounting is not about hiding profits and losses. Accounting standards must be established to provide clear, accurate, timely, and honest portrayals of a company's financial situation. No more "off balance sheet" accounting. All subsidiaries, partnerships and joint ventures must be disclosed. All officers of the corporation must disclose any involvement or investments, either direct or indirect, of any affiliated entities. Anything less is just tax fraud.

Foreclosures hurt families, communities and the moral fiber of society. Reducing interest rates to non-usurious rates will help. All foreclosures must be judicial foreclosures and whatever entity is trying to foreclose must go to court (have standing) and prove they have a right to foreclose. It is a fundamental right for everyone to have their "day in court". Our democracy depends on it.

Credit reporting bureaus and debt collectors must be controlled. The credit reporting bureaus and debt collectors have become the modern day equivalent to the slave master that cracks the whip on behalf of the plantation owner, and you know who the plantation owner is.

The credit reporting bureaus have fine tuned the art of discrimination. Redlining may be illegal, but discrimination is sanctioned. How do they compute your credit score? It is a secret that always favors the bankers; it is a secret that can't withstand the sunshine of transparency. If a lender has something negative to say about you, their word is accepted as Gospel. If you have just cause or something negative to say about a lender, your word is trash. There is nothing fair about this process. Your ability to reprove or appeal is hobbled by the structure of the system. It is not your credit report; it is controlled by the banks that pay for this system, and it is to their advantage to keep the credit scores low and charge you more because you are deemed a risk. It would be easy to say that this system should be regulated and revised, but that will take time. Justice delayed is justice denied. Protect your financial privacy. Do not allow lenders to casually access your report. Contest all inaccuracies and all derogatory entries on your credit report, and the best way to do that is with a letter that is half-printed and half-hand written – the computers can't handle these types of letters. Send lots of letters, then send some more.

The debt collectors are blood sucking scavengers. If there is a decent, honest debt collector who takes offense – too bad; you bear responsibility for not self-regulating the industry you work in. There are laws to prevent harassment and abuse from debt collectors. The first step is to write a letter to any debt collector. The next step is to contact law enforcement and demand they enforce the laws that are written to protect consumers. The next step is to ostracize debt collectors. Love the sinner but condemn the sin. Take the whip out of the slave masters hands and the plantation owner morphs from omnipotent to impotent.

Do we scold the mother who restricts her child from eating too much candy? Do we admonish a teenager for driving recklessly? Do we chastise the teacher who sets clear rules for classroom discipline? Do we punish the thief that robs a house? The answers are obvious. Nobody likes regulation: not the fat kid, the reckless teenage driver, the rowdy student, the thief, the parents, the teacher, the cop, or the judge. Still, common sense requires that brats and thieves are not the ones that establish and enforce the rules. Burdensome regulations, enforced by the heavy hand of government, are not the answer. Rules must be fair and simple, easy to recognize, follow, and enforce. Rules must be consistent and constant. For more than 4,000 years (except for the past 30 years), the most constant economic principle is to restrict usury.

Chapter 40

Step #4 – Cap Usury – 10% is Enough!

Regulation and new rules are important but the simple truth is that bankers will circumvent regulations in a haze of smoke, mirrors, and fine print; that is what has happened over the past three decades. Recent attempts to bring fairness, sanity, and consumer protections to credit cards saw the bankers cut credit limits and jack interest rates as high as 79%. The bankers are hooked on usury. They are constantly scheming to get their next fix. We have to take away their crack pipe. Pages of legalese disclosure forms won't change anything. We have to cap usury, and it must be simple enough that even government regulators can't turn it into bureaucratic fiefdoms of inefficiency.

Most states have laws against excessive usury; those laws can be enforced against you if you make a loan to a neighbor, but the banks can do whatever they want. The Depository Institutions Deregulation and Monetary Control Act (DIDMCA) of 1980 exempted federally chartered savings banks, installment plan sellers, and chartered loan companies from state usury limits. The difference between a loan shark and a banker is that the banker has a charter. DIDMCA is a failure and it needs to be challenged in court or rewritten in Congress. And even if DIDMCA is rewritten, we will still have a hodgepodge of state laws with quirky exemptions. For example, some have a general "usury limit" which is the rate that can be charged by one person or corporation to another. There might also be a legal rate which applies if you have a contractual obligation that provides simply for interest without a specific term, or "interest at the highest legal rate". In other instances, states have a "judgment rate"; that's the rate that final judgments bear. In states without a usury limit, there still may be a federally imposed limit because at certain astronomical rates of interest, "loan sharking" will be inferred by the federal government.

State laws vary. In Louisiana, the legal rate of interest is one point over the average prime rate, not to exceed 14%, nor be less than 7%. The usury limit for individuals is 12% and there is no limit for corporations. In Massachusetts, the legal rate of interest is 6%; the general usury rate is 20%. Judgments bear interest at either 12% or 18% depending on whether the court finds that a defense was frivolous. In South Dakota, the legal rate of interest is 15% and judgments bear interest at the rate of 12%. There is no other usury limit. There are certain limitations on consumer loans below $ 5,000.00. In California, the legal rate of interest is 10% for consumers; the general usury limit for non-consumers is 5% greater than the Federal Reserve Bank of San Francisco's rate. Complicated? Absolutely; the laws are so complicated that they become worthless.

Re-establishing usury limits will require either a state by state effort (South Dakota has to stop screwing the rest of America) with a challenge of interstate commerce rules that allow national banks to export usury, or a national cap on usury. The Supreme Court's *Marquette* decision said, in essence, residents of one state should not be prohibited from getting a loan from a lending institution in a different state. The decision did not prohibit a uniform national cap on usury. Uniform lending standards would enhance, not impede interstate commerce.

Usury is the largest tax on middle and working class families and the greatest transfer of wealth in history. Call it what it really is – theft – it has been a crime though out history, and it must be made a crime again to steal from hard working Americans. Opposition to usury is self defense for the poor and the poor are now the majority because of usury. A limit on usury is not an attempt to establish a new and untried theory but a return to a primary economic principle.

Usury laws, in their current form, don't protect you from the banks; they protect the banks from you. Regulation, along with new, straightforward, and enforceable, usury limits would have several positive benefits. Usury limits would help end the debt trap of credit cards. Banks would still be able to issue credit cards but they would have to pay attention to a card holders' ability to repay, and they couldn't jack up the interest rates above the usury limits. Another big benefit would be to stop the massive increase in foreclosures. When interest rates are capped, the banks would need to make responsible loans, not exotic loans that lure a borrower with low rates and then jump to ridiculous rates that lead to defaults. Usury caps on mortgage loans would also stop real estate bubbles. Remember that usury creates inflation. Caps on mortgage loans would lead to more affordable housing; predatory mortgage loans lead to foreclosure and the loss of homes; affordability leads to increased home ownership.

So, what is the appropriate cap for usury? This is a question that will surely draw debate. The appropriate and best rate is zero, absolutely no usury; but I'm not crazy either. That's not going to happen. So let's go with the real instead of the ideal.

Here is a good starting point: limit usury to a maximum 10% annual percentage rate on unsecured loans, 8% on secured loans, and a maximum 5% APR for owner occupied residential mortgage loans. These usury limits should include origination fees and other fees (the banks can't charge 10% plus fees), but should allow reasonable penalties for late payment. That still leaves existing loans that charge excessive usury; those loans will need to be modified to fit under the usury caps. If loans are not modified, the excessive usury can be taxed at 100%. Simple, easy to remember, easy to enforce.

Is 10% just an arbitrary figure? No, it is the same amount typically set aside for tithe. If 10% is good enough for God, it ought to be good enough for bankers. A 10% cap on usury would discourage speculative lending yet still reward prudent lending. When the legal rate of interest is capped, capital will flow to safe, productive purposes and not to high risk speculators. The greatest risk of default has been, and always will be, excessive usury.

A maximum of 10% would require a non-inflationary monetary policy and promote price stability. Monetary policy should be simple and consistent. Monetary policy which features wide swings in targeted interest rates inhibits financial planning and discourages investments. A cap on usury promotes moderate interest rates, stable

prices, maximum employment, and contains systemic risk in the
financial marketplace – in short, everything the Federal Reserve is
supposed to do (but doesn't), is accomplished by limiting usury.

The reason the Federal Reserve and armies of economists
can't create a stable economy is because they are wrong on the first
principle of economics. They start without a foundation – prohibitions
against usury - and then wonder why the building wobbles in a light
breeze despite their frantic manipulations. Economists hope laymen
think the dismal science is complex and difficult to comprehend. It is
not. Cap usury at 10% and the economy will experience a golden age
of prosperity; solid, steady, non-dramatic, boring, and delightful
prosperity.

So, why do we need the Fed?

Chapter 41
STEP #5 – Revoke the Fed – Why the Hell Do We Need a Middleman to Print Our Money?

Audit and then revoke the Federal Reserve.

Where did the bailout money go? The Fed refuses to answer.
How much bailout money was given away? The Fed refuses to
answer. Who got the bailout money? The Fed refuses to answer. The
Federal Reserve has never been audited by the government. If you
were trying to design a corrupt financial system, the Federal Reserve

would be your blueprint. This is a quasi-governmental agency that is not accountable to citizens, politicians, or the courts. Who does the Federal Reserve serve? Why the hell do we need a middleman to print our money?

The Constitutional role of government in monetary policy is to protect the integrity of the monetary unit and defend against counterfeiters. Congress has abdicated this responsibility. The Fed has the power to create money, by the trillions, and to give it to their banker buddies, under any terms they wish, with little or no meaningful oversight or accountability. Instead of stabilizing the economy, the Fed has destabilized it. The Fed has inflated away the value of our currency by over 96 percent since its inception. It has stolen from the poor and given to the rich through its manipulations of inflation. And now the Fed has pulled off the largest theft in history through recent bank bailouts.

The result of allowing the Fed to control the nation's monetary policy for nearly 100 years: boom, crash, boom, crash; runaway debt; endless deficits; a financial industry scam machine; a declining standard of living; near global economic meltdown. Past performance is no guarantee of future results but repeating the same mistakes and expecting a different outcome is the definition of insanity.

The Federal Reserve's main argument for its continued existence is that it is independent, meaning it is not controlled by politics. This is another way of saying they are not accountable to

American citizens; and since they can't serve two masters, the unstated implication is that they are accountable to the bankers. If Congress reclaims its Constitutional authority to control monetary policy, they will undoubtedly make mistakes, and when they do, we can guide them with our vote.

Get completely radical – follow the Constitution.

How would the government and the economy function without the Fed? We have some examples to guide us. "We issue it in proper proportion to the demands of trade and industry to make the products pass easily from the producers to the consumers. In this manner, creating for ourselves our own paper money, we control its purchasing power, and we have no interest to pay to no one." – Benjamin Franklin. Another example is when President Lincoln paid soldiers directly by printing greenback dollars.

Under the current central banking scheme, if the government decides to spend money for some worthwhile project it must first issue debt, in the form of Treasury bonds, and then sell the debt instruments to central banks, private banks, businesses, and individuals. The middlemen take their cut and charge interest. Imagine the federal government wants to spend $1 billion dollars on a project; the debt service pushes the cost to more than $2 billion over the term of a 30 year bond; that second billion, to pay the debt, adds nothing of value to the economy. Now, imagine the government cuts out the Federal Reserve, prints $1 billion in dollar bills and pays for the work as the work is done. The federal debt does not increase. The dollars printed and added to circulation do not cause inflation because there is new production for every dollar printed. The dollar is backed by production, not debt.

Debt does not build hospitals, schools, roads, bridges, post offices, or the electric grid. Treasury bonds do not build airplanes, tanks, or pay the military. Debt makes the price of everything cost more and does not add one cent to increase production. So, why the hell do we need a middleman?

Chapter 42

STEP #6 – Progressive Taxation – When the Super Rich Pay Their Fair Share, We Pay Less

If you want to catch a thief, you follow the money. Where is all the money the banks have been stealing? It's on the beach, specifically in offshore tax havens like the Cayman Islands, and the Channel Islands, and secret Swiss bank accounts.

Here is another example of how corporations are not really "persons". The US government will track US citizens everywhere to get tax money. If you leave to work in another country, you still pay US income taxes. If you still want to avoid paying your fair share of taxes, you can just give up your citizenship, right? Nope, you can't do that either. At least, you can't do it without paying a potentially

244 | Eat the Bankers

massive "exit tax". If you want to give up your citizenship, you have to give up nearly half your wealth above a certain level. Once you're gone, you're not legally allowed to come back and visit family and friends. If the government decides you have renounced citizenship for tax purposes, a federal law prohibits you from entering the country ever again. You can look up the rule under 8 USC 1182(a)(10)(E).

Corporations have regularly moved headquarters out of the US to avoid taxes. Corporations regularly shift jobs overseas and pay no taxes. The vast majority of major corporations have established offshore units to avoid taxes, often setting up hundreds of tax evading subsidiaries. This is not just a loophole in the tax code; it is plain old tax fraud. If Citigroup or Goldman Sachs wants to set up offshore accounts, they certainly can – after they pay the "exit tax", and with the understanding that re-entry by the corporation, and any subsidiary of the parent, will NEVER be permitted. Bankers cannot take the profitable entities to the tax haven and leave the unprofitable here.

The blueprint for economic growth over the past three decades has been to reduce taxes on the rich and the Corporatists; the idea being that they alone possess the unique wisdom and beneficence to invest the surplus for the greater good. They don't. They speculate and gamble with the surplus. Boom, crash, boom, crash. Clever new ways to place bets does not constitute innovation, creativity, and production.

A progressive tax makes sense, and when the Corporatists and the ultra-rich start paying their fair share and stop scamming the system, that means <u>less</u> taxes for the 99% of us that are not the ultra-wealthy.

Chapter 43

STEP #7 – Eat the Bankers – Cut Into Small Digestible Pieces and Serve with Wine

It is tempting to suggest skewering the bankers, slow roasting over an open pit of coals, and then serving with fava beans and a nice Chianti. The more sensible approach calls for cutting up the banks into small digestible pieces. Too big to fail is too dangerous to exist. According to Treasury Secretary Hank Paulson, the biggest Wall Street banks were just "too big to fail." Fed Chairman Ben Bernanke called them "systemically critical." If any of them goes down, it could take the whole financial system with it. So, taxpayers have to pay for the banks' mistakes.

Once upon a time we had antitrust laws; those laws were about more than fair pricing; they were designed to keep some corporations from becoming all powerful. The biggest banks just keep getting bigger and more dangerous; Wells Fargo acquired Wachovia; Bank of America acquired Merrill Lynch and Countrywide; JP Morgan Chase acquired Washington Mutual and Bear Stearns. Too big to fail has failed to eliminate systemic risk; it has actually made the problem bigger. The four biggest banks all have a higher ratio of troubled assets to capital reserves than before the meltdown. Wells Fargo and Citigroup have almost $3 trillion in off-balance sheet assets. JP Morgan Chase holds $79 trillion in derivative contracts. The real problem is that they are too toxic to fail, and the financial system is in a state of constant peril. While regulation of banking is certainly important, the reality is that the regulators can't keep up with the banking behemoths. The regulators may help, but they cannot prevent failure. And as the banks continue to gamble, it is inevitable they will fail and come whining for more bailout money or completely destroy the economy. Enough is enough. No single entity is indispensible. The megabanks need to be sold off in bits and pieces. The only way to manage the risk is to whittle it down to smaller pieces that can be digested in the event of failure.

Not surprisingly, the banks oppose this idea; they have sent their lobbyist out to defeat this argument. They claim they provide global services. Only the mega-banks can handle the finances of the world. They can also handle the finances of large, non-bank institutions. Multi-national corporations need mega-banks that can handle the complex transactions. Simply breaking them up - then you're discouraging a company from achieving the American Dream, working hard, earning money, producing products, and getting bigger.

Corporations don't dream, only people can dream. The truth is that when banks get too big, they choke off competition. Multiple suppliers create a more competitive market. There are no global services provided by the mega-banks that can't be provided by small to medium sized banks.

The implied threat from the mega-banks is that chopping them into small pieces will result in job losses. Bank employees will be laid off. This is a strange argument because whenever we have seen bank acquisitions and mergers, the first order of business is to fire redundant staff.

There are three more questions that must be asked: 1) Are bankers evil? 2) Is the banking system fundamentally flawed? 3) Do we need banks?

Most rank and file employees at banks are good, decent people just trying to earn a living. Some bankers are evil; they love money and that is the root of all evil. They equate money with power, and they can't comprehend that extreme inequality of money and power results in tyranny and slavery; it corrupts absolutely. They can't see that they are taking excessive gains without returning anything of value; this is the very definition of theft. They have been at the game so long; they now feel entitled to steal. The suffering they leave in their wake is cast aside with the nonchalance of a true sociopath. Usury is so bound up with injustice that its practice cannot fail to result in suffering. Some bankers will kick families to the street rather than let loose their predatory loans. "What do you think of usury? What do you think of murder?" – Cato.

Are bankers evil? Some bankers are evil incarnate.

The current banking system is based on a flawed principle. The business model is patterned after the loan shark, but on a much larger and more dangerous scale. The compounding effect of excessive usury has allowed certain banks to grow like a cancer that now infects the government and the entire economy.

On Thursday, Sept. 18, 2008, the astonished leadership of the US Congress was told in a private session by the chairman of the Federal Reserve that the American economy was in grave danger of a complete meltdown within a matter of days. There were threats of martial law. The response was to give money to the bankers that caused the near meltdown; this is roughly equivalent to giving airplanes to Al Qaeda following 9/11. Following the 9/11 attacks we all became familiar with the need for security. We dutifully remove our shoes before going to the airport gates. We allow the government to tap phone messages. We allowed the government to torture. We allowed the government to send our sons and daughters into battle and give their lives to ensure our freedom and security. When faced with destruction of the American economy, the Federal Reserve identified 19 banks that were too big to fail. The Fed guaranteed the banks with money earned from the blood and sweat of American workers, yet the government saw no need to make basic systemic changes to the banking system.

The mega-banks are so huge and interconnected that if any one were to fail all would fail. Hundreds of smaller banks have failed since the start of the financial crisis; hundreds more are expected to fail.

None of the small banks' failures threaten to meltdown the entire economy. The most obvious solution is to cut the mega-banks down, make them small enough that if one were to fail it would not destroy the entire economy.

The Constitution specifies in Article VI, clause 3 that Senators, Representatives and other elected officials must make an Oath upon taking office: "I, _____, do solemnly swear that I will support and defend the Constitution of the United States *against all enemies, foreign and domestic*; that I will bear true faith and allegiance to the same…" Where is the defense? What happened to the defenders?

Banks that threaten the entire economy are domestic enemies. Failure to chop the mega-banks into smaller, digestible pieces is tantamount to treason.

Do we need banks? Banks and money changers have been around seemingly forever. They serve a purpose but that purpose is not nearly as great as most people believe. Is there value in having a place to store money? Yes. Is there value in exchanging one currency for another to facilitate trade? Yes. Is there value in the extension of credit? Yes, but only to the extent that the debt service extracted can be overcome by the production created; excessive interest charged on debt diminishes the worth of the credit. The current banking system does provide some traditional financial services. The vast majority of the services offered are merely for the banks' own gain. To claim we need banks, in their current form, is to claim we need a cancerous tumor. The reality is that banks are a parasite on the economy and the sooner they're removed, the sooner we can hope to see a sustainably healthy economy. Of course, removing a cancer is dangerous and painful. When banks are cut out of the economy, the change will be difficult for many. The alternative is to leave the cancer in place; this option will kill the host – maybe not today, maybe not tomorrow, but inevitably.

Chapter 44

STEP #8 – Cut the National Debt – To Get Out of a Hole, You've Got to Stop Digging

The US is the most indebted nation in history. On July 30th 2009, US Government debt totaled $11.7 trillion, or roughly $38,000 for every man, woman, and child in the country. We are $1.5 trillion poorer than we were one year ago. In another 12 months we will be $2 trillion deeper in debt. Total US debt including government, consumers and corporations is $52 trillion - or about $600,000 for every family of 4. Total issued US debt of $52 trillion does not count US derivates ($253 trillion) or government guarantees for bank and brokerage accounts, pensions and Medicare. Unfunded government IOUs are also coming due on Social Security, Medicare, and Federal pension payments; those obligations are enormous; an estimated $104 trillion.

The size of the bailout so far, is absolutely unprecedented in all of history. Bailout spending, adjusted for inflation, equals the cost of the Marshall Plan, Louisiana Purchase, S&L Crisis, Korean War, New Deal, Iraq invasion, Vietnam, and NASA – combined. Only World War II rivaled the bailout, but the bailout continues to grow.

If we assume a national debt of $52 trillion with interest payments at 5%, the annual interest per family would be $30,000. The average household income is approximately $50,000 per year. It is unrealistic to pay the debt out of income. But this debt must be liquidated somehow. It is impossible to borrow and spend, or tax and spend our way out of this debt. This year and every year for the foreseeable future, Washington will have to borrow 80% of the world's surplus savings just to pay its bills. We owe more to foreign investors, retirees and ordinary citizens than we could ever hope to repay. Government is good at borrowing, not so good at repaying. The nation will have to walk away from our debts.

How does a nation walk away from its debt? The most common path is to debase or devalue the currency in an attempt to service and repay their debt with cheaper money. This is a last ditch effort but fairly common; it has happened in Russia, Brazil, Argentina, France, Austria the United Kingdom, and the United States (under FDR and later under Nixon). The devaluation process is painful. In the past, the currency was devalued relative to gold. Now that the dollar is no longer tied to gold, formal proclamations are not required. The devaluation process now happens whenever the Federal Reserve cranks up the printing press. The Fed starts printing whenever the government issues new debt. There is a lot of new debt required to keep the economy floating. The results are the same as devaluation. The dollar buys less. The cost of living jumps. Bankruptcies happen with ever increasing frequency. Economic growth sputters. When devaluation occurs quickly, the result is known as a crack-up boom. Inflation skyrockets and your savings disappear. When devaluation is dragged out, it is still painful. The destruction of our incomes, our savings, our investments and our retirements is the most personal financial crisis any of us will ever have to deal with. It is also the greatest theft in history. You might want to send a thank you note to the Corporatist politicians, Republicans and Democrats, and the bankers. Maybe not.

Will the US devalue the dollar? It is inevitable. The only question is whether it will be quick or slow. Debt has destroyed all the major empires in history. Debt matters. The largest national debt in history is definitely abnormal. We can delay the inevitable by printing more dollars, but eventually there will be a reckoning, a reversion to the mean, a return to normal – or at least a new normal. So, how can we deal with the debt, and relieve at least some of the suffering, and maybe (with a little luck) still enjoy some prosperity?

If you are in a hole and you want to get out of the hole, the first rule is to stop digging. We know that usury compounds and grows exponentially. By cutting usury we can shrink the size of the hole; we might just have a fighting chance.

Chapter 45

STEP #9 – Cut Personal Debt – Break the Chains of Debt: Payback is a Bitch

Live frugally. Save as much as possible. Do not take on new debt. Don't spend money you don't have.

Taking on debt is like getting a tattoo. It won't go away on its own, and getting rid of it can be painful. There are three ways to cast off existing debt: pay it off, negotiate, or default.

Paying off debt can be a fairly simple act for some people or an enormous challenge for others, but it requires conscious action. You need to identify your debt, income, and expenses. You need to put this information on paper, include all the information, and develop a game plan. If you can increase your income and/or decrease your expenses, you may be able to pay down your debts. For many people the obligation to pay debt is a moral issue; for others it is a practical issue; for everyone it is a personal issue.

If you are unable to reconcile payment on your debts, then the next consideration is to negotiate with your creditors. Many credit card companies are willing to accept 30 or 40 cents on the dollar. Individuals can negotiate directly credit card companies. Debt consolidation companies may be able to provide some assistance but typically they just repackage the debt, and the new package may be more onerous than the old mess of debt; use caution and skepticism, or just avoid debt consolidators. The biggest debt for most people is a home mortgage. Loan modifications can help but they can also hurt. By mid-2009, only 8% of delinquent mortgages were being modified, and almost two-thirds of the modifications were non-concessionary; that means the debt was not reduced; late payments and fees were tacked onto the back of the mortgage or the mortgage term was extended, and sometimes the monthly payments actually increased. Concessionary modifications typically lowered the monthly payment, or the interest rate, or on rare occasions actually lowered the principal amount of the mortgage.

An option to mortgage modification is the strategic default, and there are two versions. If you want to stay in your current home but you are facing negative equity, then you might consider selling the property in a short sale to a family member, friend, or friendly investor (possibly in the form of an LLC); they turn around and lease the property back to you with an option to buy. It may take some time to be able to exercise the option. The strategic short sale is a default and will be considered a severe negative on credit reports. The advantage is that the original homeowner does not have to move, and it may wipe out the negative equity.

The other version of a strategic default is to just stop paying. It normally takes at least 3 months before a homeowner can be evicted (varies from state to state) and if you communicate with the loan servicers you can probably stall for a few extra months. If you attempt a short sale during this time, you could stall for several more months. A more aggressive approach is to challenge the validity of the original mortgage on grounds of violations of truth in lending laws, RESPA, or the holder in due course of the note; there were many lending violations over the past few years and if your rights were violated you might even go to court. Your chances of winning a court battle are miniscule; your chances of stalling a foreclosure are good. At some point you will almost certainly be evicted. Rep. Marcy Kaptur had the courage tell her constituents that they should refuse eviction. If the Sherriff evicts, move back in; be squatters in your own home; don't leave – always in a peaceful and non-violent manner.

While the default process is happening you may be able to find another house for a far lower price. Here is a real example: a homeowner purchased a house in 2006 for $325,000 with a mortgage of $292,500. By late 2009, the house had a market value of $125,000. The homeowner defaulted on the mortgage and then co-signed on a new mortgage with family members to purchase a comparable home in the same area for $85,000. The move eliminated $207,500 in debt, which over the term of the mortgage would have cost more than $496,000 (at 7%); that's money the homeowner could either pay to the banks, or save for their children's education, healthcare, living expenses, and retirement.

The government, the banks, the credit bureaus, and the media are all telling us that not paying your mortgage makes you a bad person; it is a reflection of our morality and honor. We are brainwashed into believing that our credit score is a measure of our human worth. Foreclosure only happens to loathsome, vile creatures. The campaign to get you to pay the mortgage is well orchestrated and ubiquitous. When the exhortations are exhausted, the threats begin. The stigma will linger for a lifetime. You will have to sew a scarlet letter on all your sweaters. If you don't pay, your credit score will be slammed. You won't be able to get credit. You won't be able to buy another house. You won't be able to buy a car. You won't be able to rent a car. You're unfit to ride in a car. Take your place at the back of the bus.

This may be the most twisted irony in recent history. The bankers are calling their customers immoral. What's next? Satan calls jaywalkers evil.

The real double standard is revealed when we see what bankers do when they have difficulty paying their own mortgage. In 2010, a joint venture between Tishman Speyer and Blackrock defaulted on an apartment project in New York. The investment bankers had a $5.6 billion dollar mortgage; unable to refinance, they walked away from property that was worth $1.8 billion, leaving a deficit of $3.8 billion. Investors in the mortgage included California state pension plans, the state of Florida, and the Church of England. The $3.8 billion dollar deficit equaled the mortgages of more than 27,000 houses. Nothing personal, it's just business.

There are two parties to a mortgage contract; you and the bank. When a bank loses money, they write down the loss, get a tax break, ship jobs offshore, transfer the loss off the balance sheet, collect a big bonus, and get bailed out by taxpayers. The bankers are not constrained by morals; they are profit driven machines. When a homeowner loses money on a house, they become the devil's spawn. The time has come to stand up for your rights and treat the bankers they same way they treat you. Bankers have been shafting the public, now they should be hoisted on their own petard. Payback is a bitch.

In addition to the "demand the note" defense and the "predatory lending practices" defense, there are two more legal concepts which apply to the homeowner considering default. "Efficient breach" holds that it is ethical to breach a contract in cases where the consequences for default are less harmful to than the consequences of adhering to the contract. In other words, contract law recognizes that deals can go bad, and it is better to break a contract than allow the terms of the contract to destroy you. The other legal concept applies in states with non-deficiency statutes, such as California and Arizona, where lenders have a right to foreclose on the home but may not pursue other legal claims against the borrower. Default and subsequent foreclosure are considered valid fulfillment of the mortgage contract; therefore lenders don't have the legal right to report mortgage defaults to credit bureaus, and default should not have a negative effect on the borrower's credit score. You will most probably need to defend that credit score against invalid negative reports.

A contract is a legally binding agreement between two parties setting forth mutually agreeable terms of a transaction. Every mortgage loan contract includes default and foreclosure as a possible outcome, and in many instances default may be the most appropriate, sensible, and ethical solution to fulfill the contract.

What would happen if everybody who is underwater stopped making their mortgage payments? The economy would prosper. Home prices would drop to very affordable levels. Money that is being sucked into the banks' coffers would instead be spent by consumers. The money would be a huge economic stimulus. Better yet, some of the money might be saved, tucked away for the future, eliminating the need for future indebtedness.

The other way to eliminate debt is through bankruptcy. The idea of bankruptcy goes back to Biblical times when every 49 years, on the year of Jubilee, all debts were wiped out. More than 2000 years ago, people understood that debt could become an inescapable trap; for many people the only way to get a fresh start was Jubilee. Now, bankruptcy offers a fresh start. The restrictions on bankruptcy have never been tougher, but it is still possible. The important thing to remember is that once you get a fresh start you should be diligent to avoid falling back in the debt trap.

For many people, the decision of how to deal with debt boils down to a choice between money for personal survival and the well being of your family, or paying off the bankers. Whatever path you take be sure to follow your conscience. Walking away might be the most morally responsible choice. So far, the bankers have controlled homeowners through fear and loathing, and we have played our role as subservient sheeple; cowering, scared, and ashamed. The bankers are not going to change voluntarily, and if the current condition continues, the economy will suffer for years to come. If enough people walk away, we might just reach a tipping point where the bankers are forced to respond with equity and fairness. Fear mongering is not the solution.

Chapter 46

STEP #10 – Clog the Machine – Fight Back: If You Do Nothing, Nothing Changes

What would Jesus do about usury? We have a pretty good idea. We know he chased the money changers from the temple. He used a whip. He threw tables. He violently attacked the usurers. The most forgiving soul never forgave the money lenders. I don't think we should follow the Prince of Peace's example. I suggest non-violent civil disobedience.

If you do nothing, nothing will change. The laws of logic have not changed and you can trace premises to their logical conclusion, and if we stay on our current path we will surely arrive at a painful conclusion; the most probable outcome is a failed economy and great suffering for all but the elite few. Conscience remains alert to condemn wrong and approve right. The condemnation of usury prevailed for most of recorded history. Usury was evil 4,000 years ago; it is evil today. Conscience has not changed over the ages, but conscience must be enlightened, or made intelligent by reason and logic to enable it to find the right decision.

Civil disobedience is the process of heading toward enlightenment through deliberate violation of commands, demands, policies, or laws of those in authority – always in a non-violent and peaceful manner. The purpose of civil disobedience can be to publicize an unjust law or condition; or to publicize a just cause; to appeal to the conscience of the public; to push negotiation or consideration; to challenge legal standing in court; to end your own complicity in the injustice which flows from obedience to unjust laws. Do not cooperate – clog the machine.

If you realize that usury is the root cause of great injustice, then you have a duty to at least wash your hands of it, and withdraw your support for it, and accept personal responsibility. Just reading this book is an act of civil disobedience; discussing the injustice of usury is a bolder act; raising your voice in opposition is an even better act; breaking a few rules is better yet – always in a non-violent and peaceful manner. Voluntarily becoming unbanked, as much as possible, is an act of disobedience. Switching your bank account to a small community bank or credit union and out of the hands of a mega bank is an act of civil disobedience. You can fire your bank. Take the money out of the hands of the big bankers and see if smaller, local, community oriented firms can be a better warehouse for your savings. In a society that wallows in debt, paying cash can be a subtle yet worthwhile act of civil disobedience. And not paying usurious debt is an extremely powerful tool of civil disobedience.

Vilifying bankers is important. It is inherent in their business. We have always held bankers in severe disrepute and deservedly so; from the money changers in the temple to the Lombards in Holland; from Shylock in Venice to the fat cats on Wall Street. Vilification is the only thing the bankers have honestly earned, because they break the public trust. The public trusted that bankers would be honest stewards of their deposits. The banks trusted the borrowers would repay their loans. This was always the pact; it was a burden that served a purpose. The trust was violated by the bankers who embraced usury in its myriad forms: predatory loans, leverage, fractional reserves, and derivatives. Without vilification and consequences for the violation of trust, the system falls apart. It happened in the 1930's and there were runs on banks. Only when customers demanded cash did they learn their deposits had been stolen. Usury is theft and accepting and rewarding usury is the moral equivalent of buying stolen merchandise. One of the most important and meaningful acts of civil disobedience is to default on usurious debt. Vilification is not a call for blood but a recognition that the bankers have cheated, and a demand for honesty. The bankers refuse to be held accountable for their actions; vilification places blame at their feet.

Goldman Sachs CEO, Lloyd Blankfein acknowledged the growing resentment, "I know I could slit my wrists and people would cheer." Americans would not cheer bank executives' deaths because we are ugly and mean spirited; to the contrary, we are generally charitable, compassionate, and forgiving. We would cheer because we know, in our collective marrow, that the financial system is rotten to the core, even if most people can't define the root cause of the infection – usury. We would cheer like slaves breaking free of their chains and basking in the sunshine of freedom. The bankers will try to suppress insurrection. They will choke the flow of money. They will evict people to the streets. They will grind the economy to a standstill. They will blame the child from accepting candy from a molester. They understand that the best defense is a strong offense.

The Corporatists have orchestrated a campaign of fear in order to keep the rabble in line. The government and the media extol the virtue of paying all debts, even predatory and usurious loans. There is a stigma attached to default, but there is also a stigma attached to being penniless without a roof over your head; the former helps alleviate the latter. We are no longer citizens, we are consumers. We are the slaves and the lenders are the slave masters. Thoreau warned us that many people believe the proper response to unjust conditions is to try to use the political process to change the law, while obeying and respecting the law until it is changed. However, if the law is clearly unjust, and the legislative process does not address the injustice, then the law deserves no respect. Slavery was once legal, but it was unjust and morally wrong. Slaves broke the law when they tried to escape.

Abolitionists broke the law trying to free slaves. The greater crime is doing nothing in the face of injustice. Thoreau realized that not everyone could battle injustice but almost anyone could do something to clog the machine.

You serve your country poorly if you suppress your conscience in favor of the law. If you allow yourself to be treated like sheep, you will be. If you live in fear, you will be oppressed. Your rights are not inalienable; they can be taken from you. Your freedom is not guaranteed; you must demand it and guard it. Thomas Jefferson may have said it best: "When the people fear their government, there is tyranny; when the government fears the people, there is liberty."

What can you do? There is no set answer. Rosa Parks took her seat in the front of a segregated bus. She had been working all day and her feet hurt and there were no seats in the back of the bus. She did not try to change history but she did. There will probably come a time, a place, a fleeting moment in your life when you are tired of giving in. Peacefully take your seat at the front of the bus and don't be afraid.

Chapter 47

STEP #11 – Stimulate the Economy – You Know How to Spend Your Money Better Than the Bankers

The US economy freed of usury, will grow as never before. We have at least one blueprint in the GI Bill. When servicemen returned from World War II, they were given the opportunity to buy homes with low and reasonable interest rates; homeownership exploded. The American middle class was the envy of the world. The GI Bill was the greatest, most powerful stimulus package in American history.

Each unit of interest paid reduces the utility, or usefulness, of a loan, which leads to a reduction in usefulness to the overall economy. Each unit of interest paid decreases overall prosperity. There is an inverse relationship between high interest rates and prosperity; high interest rates creates negative prosperity. The capital needed to improve the standard of living is lost in the payment of interest on debts. Those who argue that usury leads to an improvement for the economy should offer proof of that improvement, but that proof has never been proved. The banks have been bleeding us dry for so long that we have become blind to the reality that debt is debt and wealth is wealth. A person with $100 of debt is not wealthier than a person with $90 of cash. The opposite is true. The prosperity enjoyed in the US is not the result of usurious debt but of hard work and production. Households and nations, freed of debt, prosper. When usury is capped, speculation and gambling will not be rewarded so richly, but investment will continue to draw the attention of capital. The evidence is overwhelming.

Given the opportunity, Americans will start small businesses. We know that 65% of all new jobs are created by small businesses. We will seek training and education. We'll tinker and invent. Some guy in a garage in Wichita or Ventura will build a car to get 200 miles per gallon. A woman working in a small laboratory will find a cure to cancer. We can create renewable, sustainable, clean energy sources. We can cure diseases. We can improve our schools. We can rebuild our bridges and dams. We can care for our elders. If we must go to war, we will refuse to leave our bravest heroes unprotected, and when they come home we will honor our commitments to them. We can do all this and more, or we can continue to let the bankers steal through usury; taking a cut of everything without producing anything.

It would take an army of economists to calculate the savings from capping usury. In the late 1970's, the financial sector accounted for approximately 16% of corporate domestic profits. By 2007, the financial sector accounted for approximately 41% of corporate domestic profits. The 25% difference between the 1970s and 2007 can be attributed primarily to usury. Imagine taking that 25% profit and plowing it back into the economy for productive purposes. The financial sector accounts for approximately 31% of the GDP, up from 20% in the 1970s. That difference, attributed primarily to usury, represents more than $1.5 trillion and is a good estimate of the potential stimulus.

We know that capping bank fees would save tens of billions per year; capping excessive interest rates could easily save hundreds of billions of dollars per year. Avoiding more bank bailouts could save hundreds of billions more. The savings from capping usury are probably enough to balance the federal budget and pay down the national debt. The savings from capping usury would also redirect money to the best, most productive uses.

Some people will argue that investment capital will dry up if there is a cap on usury, but the truth is that investment capital will continue to be invested. A cap on usury would provide incentive to create businesses, an incentive for people with money to invest – not speculate, but invest – the money in productive business. It is preposterous to imagine that people with investment capital will sit on their wallets. The money will circulate through the economy, and create jobs, and produce value. The money would be in your hands, not the bankers. No single act or package would stimulate the economy more, and have a more sustainable impact on the economy, than a cap on usury.

The radical experiment in destroying consumer protections against excessive usury failed. If you want a stable economy without crazy boom and bust cycles that threaten the economic security of the nation; if you want low and stable inflation; if you want to increase affordable home ownership; if you want to bring back "Made in America"; if you want to increase employment; if you want a vibrant and robust middle class; if you want banks to stop gambling and start providing honest banking service; if you want the dollar to remain strong; if you want America to remain strong; and if you have had enough of the wealthy, elite Corporatists trying to destroy democracy and bankrupt your family – then 10 percent is enough.

So far, $12.2 trillion has been committed to bailouts; up to $23 trillion has been earmarked if needed. Still, $12.2 trillion is a staggering figure. To put it in perspective it works out to about $40,000 for every person in America or about $2,033 dollars for ever human on the planet. Approximately 3 billion people live on less than $2.50 per day, or less than $913 per year. One billion people live on less than a dollar a day, or less than $365 per year. Passing out $2,033 to every human on the planet would be nearly impossible and even if you did give out the money, much of it would fall into the wrong hands or otherwise be squandered – but you have to think that a whole lot of that money would help a whole lot of people; in a best case scenario it could wipe out many preventable diseases, feed the hungry, and eliminate poverty.

But that's not happening; we are not eliminating poverty, death, and misery; instead, the money will go to bankers.

Of course, we never got a chance to vote on whether we would like to eliminate hunger, preventable diseases, and poverty in our lifetime – or give the money to bankers. We never got a chance to vote on whether we wanted to spend taxpayer dollars to prop up Wall Street gambling, or to put the money back in the hands of Main Street families and businesses. We never got a chance to vote on bailout money for bankers or taking the same dollars and installing solar panels on every house in the world. In the time it took you to read this page, 15 children have died of hunger-related causes, and 14 Americans lost their home to foreclosure. Trillions of dollars can continue to go to the bankers or the money can be returned to the rightful owners, the 99% of Americans who will use that money with willing hands of practical purpose. You know how to spend your money better than the bankers.

A choice is being made and that choice will be the lasting legacy of this generation.

Chapter 48

STEP #12 - Go Forth!

Prohibitions against usury work. Usury results in financial and societal failure. The prohibition against usury is supported by the greatest minds in history. The prohibition against usury is a primary economic principle. An error does not become truth through repetition, nor does truth become an error because it is forgotten. The prohibition against usury is not an untried experiment.

For readers who believe in God the message is clear, regardless of your religious affiliation. We have been told over the ages that usury is a sin. You may take exception. You may think that divine wisdom established centuries ago does not apply to modern economics.

You may think God is wrong.

Or, perhaps we are wrong to allow usury. Perhaps we should go back to the original Word and try His way again.

Oppression and injustice must ultimately and inevitably fail. Truth must always eventually prevail. Any sustainably successful economic system must be based principles of equity, fairness, justice, opportunity for prosperity, and compassion for one another. Usury lacks any foundation to build an economic system.

There is a long history of subjugation, exploitation, and oppression of the great majority of people by an elite few. Oppression can come in many forms: monarchy, oligarchy, fascism, dictatorship, corporatism, and more. Those in positions of power employ experts to legitimize and justify their oppression; fear is a strong motivating factor, fear that things could be worse, either at the hands of the oppressors or some unknown force. The fears of the elite are inevitably revealed as frailty and weakness over time. Hope is much more powerful than fear. Hope never dies; it grows stronger in the face of oppression. History has proved that systems and regimes built on oppression and injustice always fail in time, always.

Having been enlightened, carry this message to others who have felt the injustice of usury and take action to free yourself and others from the chains of debt.

We are on a road to progress not perfection. The next step is yours.

APPENDIX

Scriptural References to Usury – King James Version

Exodus 20:10
10 But the seventh day is the Sabbath of the Lord they God: *in it* thou shalt not do any work, thou, nor thy son, nor thy daughter, thy manservant, nor thy cattle, nor thy stranger that *is* within thy gates:

Exodus 20:15
15 Thou shalt not steal.

Exodus 22:25-27
25 If thou lend money to *any of* my people *that is* poor by thee, thou shalt not be to him as an usurer, neither shalt thou lay upon him usury.
26 If thou at all take they neighbor's raiment to pledge, thou shalt deliver it unto him by that the su goeth down:
27 For that *is* his covering only, it *is* his raiment for his skin: Wherein shall he sleep? And it shall come to pass, when he crieth unto me, that I will hear: for I *am* gracious.

Leviticus 19:33, 34
33 And if a stranger sojourn with thee in your land, ye shall not vex him.
34 *But* the stranger that dwelleth with you shall be unto you as one born among you, and thou shalt love him as thyself; for ye were strangers in the land of Egypt. I *am* the Lord your God.

Leviticus 23:22
22 And when ye reap the harvest of the land, thou shalt not make clean riddance of the corners of thy field when thou reapest, neither shalt thou gather any gleaning of thy harvest: thou shalt leave them unto the poor and to the stranger: I *am* the Lord your God.

Leviticus 25:8-14

8 And thou shalt number seven Sabbaths of years unto thee, seven times seven years; and the space of the seven Sabbaths of years shall be unto forty and nine years.

9 Then shalt thou cause the trumpet of the jubilee to sound on the tenth *day* of the seventh month, in the day of atonement shall ye make the trumpet sound throughout *all* your land.

10 And ye shall hallow the fiftieth year and proclaim liberty throughout all the land unto all the inhabitants thereof: it shall be a jubilee unto you: and ye shall return every man unto his possession, and ye shall return every man unto his family.

11 A jubilee shall that fiftieth year be unto you: ye shall not sow, neither reap that which growth of itself in it, nor gather *the grapes* in it of thy vine undressed.

12 For it *is* the jubilee; it shall be holy unto you: ye shall eat the increase thereof out of the field.

13 In the year of this jubilee ye shall return every man unto his possession.

14 And if thou sell ought unto thy neighbor, or buyest *ought* of thy neighbour's hand, ye shall not oppress one another.

Leviticus 25:35-37

35 And if thy brother be waxen poor, and fallen in decay with thee; then thou shalt relieve him: *yea, though he be* a stranger, or a sojourner; that he may live with thee.

36 Take thou no usury of him, or increase: but fear thy God; that thy brother may live with thee.

37 Thou shalt not give him thy money upon usury, nor lend him thy victuals for increase.

Leviticus 27:30

30 And all the tithe of the land, whether of the seed of the land, or of the fruit of the tree, is the Lord's: it is holy unto the Lord.

Deuteronomy 15:1-4

1 At the end of *every* seven years thou shalt make a release.

2 And this is the manner of the release: Every creditor that lendeth *ought* unto his neighbor shall release *it*; he shall not exact *it* of his

neighbor, or of his brother: because it is called the Lord's release;
3 Of a foreigner thou mayest exact *it again*: but *that* which is thine
with thy brother thine hand shall release;
4 Save when there shall be no poor among you; for the Lord shall
gretly bless thee in the land which the Lord they God giveth the *for* an
inheritance to possess it:

Deuteronomy 15:7-9
7 If there be among you a poor man of one of thy brethren within any
of thy gates in thy land which the Lord thy God giveth thee, thou shalt
not harden thine heart, nor shut thine hand from thy poor brother:
8 But thou shalt open thine hand wide unto him, and thou shalt surely
lend him sufficient for his need, in *that* which he wanteth.
9 Beware that there be not a thought in thy wicked heart, saying, The
seventh year, the year of release, is at hand: and thine eye be evil
against thy poor brother, and thou givest him nought: and he cry unto
the Lord against thee, and it be a sin unto thee.

Deuteronomy 15:15
15 And thou shalt remember that thou wast a bondman in the land of
Egypt, and the Lord thy God redeemed thee: therefore I command thee
this thing to day.

Deuteronomy 23:19
19 Thou shalt not lend upon usury to thy brother; usury of money,
usury of victuals, usury of any thing that is lent upon usury:

Deuteronomy 23:20
20 Unto a stranger thou mayest lend upon usury; but unto thy brother
thou shalt not lend upon usury: that the Lord thy God may bless thee
in all that thou settest thine hand to in the land whither thou goest to
possess it.

II Chronicles 31:4
4 Moreover he commanded the people that dwelt in Jerusalem to give
the portion of the priests and the Levites, that they might be
encouraged in the law of the Lord.

Nehemiah 5:6-7
6 And I was very angry when I heard their cry and these words.
7 Then I consulted with myself, and I rebuked the nobles, and the rulers, and said unto them, Ye exact usury, every one of his brother. And I set a great assembly against them.

Nehemiah 5:9-13
9 Also I said, It *is* not good that ye do: ought ye not to walk in the fear of our God because of the reproach of the heathen our enemies?
10 I likewise, *and* my brethren, and my servants, might exact of them money and corn: I pray you, let us leave off this usury.
11 Restore, I pray you, to them, even this day, their lands, their vineyards, their oliveyards, and their houses, also the hundredth *part* of the money, and of the corn, the wine, and the oil, that ye exact of them.
12 Then said they, We will restore *them*, and will require nothing of them; so will we do as thou sayest. Then I called the priests, and took an oath of them, that they should do according to this promise.
13 Also I shook my lap, and said, So God shake out every man from his house, and from his labour, that performeth not this promise, even thus be he shaken out, and emptied. And all the congregation said, Amen, and praised the Lord. And the people did according to this promise.

Psalm 15:5
5 *He that* putteth not out his money to usury, nor taketh reward against the innocent. He that doeth these *things* shall never be moved.

Proverbs 22:7-9
7 The rich ruleth over the poor, and the borrower is servant to the lender.
8 He that soweth iniquity shall reap vanity: and the rod of his anger shall fail
9 He that hath a bountiful eye shall be blessed: for he giveth his bread to the poor.

Proverbs 22:16
16 He that oppresseth the poor to increase his *riches*, *and* he that giveth to the rich, *shall* surely *come* to want.

Proverbs 22:22
22 Rob not the poor, because he *is* poor: neither oppress the afflicted in the gate:

Proverbs 28:8
8 He that by usury and unjust gain increaseth his substance, he shall gather it for him that will pity the poor.

Isaiah 10:15
15 Shall the axe boast itself against him that heweth therewith? *or* shall the saw magnify itself against him that shaketh it? As if the rod should shake *itself* against them that lift it up, *or* as if the staff should lift up *itself, as if it were* no wood.

Isaiah 24:1, 2
1 Behold, the Lord maketh the earth empty, and maketh it waste, and turneth it upside down, and scattereth abroad the inhabitants thereof.
2 And it shall be, as with the people, so with the priest; as with the servant, so with his master; as with the maid, so with her mistress; as with the buyer, so with the seller; as with the lender, so with the borrower; as with the taker of usury, so with the giver of usury to him.

Jeremiah 15:10
10 Woe is me, my mother, that thou hast borne me a man of strife and a man of contention to the whole earth! I have neither lent on usury, nor men have lent to me on usury; *yet* every one of them doth curse me.

Ezekiel 18:7-9
7 And hath not oppressed any, *but* hath restored to the debtor his pledge, hath spoiled none by violence, hath given his bread to the hungry, and hath covered the naked with a garment;
8 He *that* hath not given forth upon usury, neither hath taken any increase, *that* hath withdrawn his hand from iniquity, hath executed true judgment between man and man,
9 Hath walked in my statutes, and hath kept my judgments, to deal truly; he *is* just, he shall surely live, saith the Lord God.

Ezekiel 18:13

13 Hath given forth upon usury, and hath taken increase: shall he then live? he shall not live: he hath done all these abominations; he shall surely die; his blood shall be upon him.

Ezekiel 18:17

17 *That* hath taken off his hand from the poor, *that* hath not received usury nor increase, hath executed my judgments, hath walked in my statutes: he shall not die for the iniquity of his father, he shall surely live.

Ezekiel 22:12

12 In thee have they taken gifts to shed blood; thou hast taken usury and increase, and thou hast greedily gained of thy neighbours by extortion, and hast forgotten me, saith the Lord God.

Matthew 6:12

12 "And forgive us our debts, as we forgive our debtors,"

Matthew 6:24

24 "No man can serve two masters; for either he will hate the one and love the other; or else he will hold to the one, and despise the other. Ye cannot serve God and mammon."

Matthew 21:12, 13

12 And Jesus went into the temple of God, and cast out all of them that sold and bought in the temple, and overthrew the tables of the moneychangers, and the seats of them that sold doves,
13 And he said unto them, "It is written, My house shall be called a house of prayer; but ye have made it a den of thieves."

Matthew 23:23

23 "Woe unto you, scribes and Pharisees, hypocrites! for ye pay tithe of mint and anise and cumin, and have omitted the weightier *matters* of the law, judgment, mercy, and faith: these ought ye to have done, and not to leave the other undone."

Matthew 25:27
27 "Thou oughtest therefore to have put my money to the exchangers, and *then* at my coming I should have received mine own with usury."

Matthew 25:26-29
26 "His lord answered and said to him, Thou wicked and slothful servant, thou knewest that I reap where I sowed not, and gather where I have not strawed.
27 Thou oughtest therefore to have put my money to the exchangers, and then at my coming I should have received mine own with usury.
28 Take therefore the talent from him, and give it unto him which hath ten talents."

Luke 6:34, 35
34 "And if ye lend *to them* of whom ye hope to receive, what thank have ye? for sinners also lend to sinners, to receive as much again."
35 "But love ye your enemies, and do good, and lend, hoping for nothing again; and your reward shall be great, and ye shall be the children of the Highest: for he is kind unto the unthankful and *to* the evil."

Luke 19:21-26
21 "For I feareth thee, because thou art an austere man: thou takest up that thou layedst not down, and reapest that thou didst not sow."
22 "And he saith unto him, Out of your own mouth will I judge thee, *thou* wicked servant. Thou knewest that I was an austere man, taking up that I laid not down, and reaping that I did not sow."
23 "Wherefore then gavest not thou my money ionto a bank, that at my coming I might have required mine won with usury?"
24 "And he said unto them that stood by, Take from him the pound, and give *it* to him that hath ten pounds."
25 "(And they said unto him, Lord, he hath ten pounds.)"
26 "For I say to you, That unto every one which hath shall be given; and from him that hath not, even that he hath shall be taken away from him."

John 2:15
15 And when he had made a scourge of small cords, he drove them all

out of the temple, and the sheep and the oxen; and poured out the changers' money, and overthrew the tables;

Romans 13:8
8 Owe no man any thing, but to love one another: for he that loveth another hath fulfilled the law.

About the Author:

Sinclair Noe is the former host of the "Financial Review" and is the editor of Bank-o-Meter.com. He is a respected financial analyst. He is the author of four books on investing and economics. Noe is an estate planner currently living in Phoenix, Arizona.

www.ingramcontent.com/pod-product-compliance
Lightning Source LLC
Chambersburg PA
CBHW071401170526
45165CB00001B/138